Edited by GUSTAVE L. WEINSS

With the Editor

Every-Day Lessons How many, I wonder, take into account the daily happenings, big or little, and try to learn from them the lessons they point out? Scarcely is there an incident that does not contain some food for thought, a lesson that will mean for us much profit if we but heed it.

The banker studies the trend of events and the business that comes to his doors—the demand for money, the collateral offered as security for loans, the savings of depositors—and he knows almost to a certainty just how he may proceed.

The merchant studies the demand for his wares and knows what lines are safe for him to deal in and what ones are not.

The executive studies the habits and character of his associates and learns on whom he can depend.

But greater yet are the lessons to be learned from the common, every-day events that happen, for they carry with them stories by which every individual can profit.

Observe, if you please, how those with whom you are acquainted, and even those whom you do not know, conduct themselves in times of fortune or misfortune, in times of adversity or success, when tempted and when not tempted. Also, reason out for yourself just what you would do under similar circumstances. Then you will arrive at definite conclusions, and just what these are will go a long way toward making you an undesirable member of your community or one who will be looked up to as a person that others would like to emulate.

Be a Little Kinder A few days ago I ran across a little poem that impressed me so much that I should like to have you read it, think about it, and put it into practice. Read it:

Let me be a little kinder,
Let me be a little blinder
To the faults of those about me;
Let me praise a little more;
Let me be when I am weary
Just a little bit more cheery—
Let me serve a little better
Those that I am striving for.

Think about it. Doesn't it make you wish you hadn't said what you did about some one the other day? Doesn't it make you feel that in the future you are going to be more tolerant, that you are going to place credit where credit is due and even seek a chance to offer praise, that you are going to do what you can to make things brighter for your associates, that you are going to be more cheerful in your efforts to serve yourself and others?

If it makes you feel that way, do try to put it into practice every day.

I like the thoughts this little poem contains, for I know that kindness is a golden chain that binds us all closer together; that toleration is the real test of character—the test that shows whether we are big or petty; that praise, whether one has been successful or not, so long as one has tried, encourages success; that cheerfulness makes bearable conditions that seem unbearable; and that honest effort has its own reward in the satisfaction that comes to us in having done our best.

Christmas in Your Heart Each year as the holiday of holidays approaches, I wonder whether there really is any one who fails to be carried away with the spirit of Christmas. It just seems that no matter where you look or where you go, you see some one planning or preparing to make some one else glad.

Surely it would be an interesting experience if we could look into every heart at this time. I am positive we would find every one brimful of Christmas, and by this I mean gladness, for, after all, Christmas is but a synonym for gladness.

And why should we not rejoice? Is not Christmas the birthday of our Saviour? Nothing should be allowed to prevent us from doing all we can, in His name, to relieve the hungry, to cheer the sorrowing, to brighten the depressed, to make more glad the glad. Nothing should deter us from giving of our store to the poor and the needy, the children, and our friends.

In so doing, we, too, will benefit, for every time we make some one else happy we increase our own happiness. We swell the Christmas in our hearts and come to the possession of a good conscience, the kind that Franklin meant when he said, "A good conscience is a continual Christmas."

So my best wish for you during the coming holidays is that you will allow Christmas to dwell in your heart, for once it is there it will remain with you—and you will surely let it—for all time to come.

The Spirit of *Prayer*

By MARY BROOKS PICKEN
Director of Instruction

ALWAYS there is a quiet sweetness that comes into my heart when it is prayer time in church, or when I hear little folks' goodnight prayers, or whenever I recognize that I am in the presence of the Spirit of Prayer.

> Prayer is the heart's sincere desire,
> Uttered or unexpressed,
> The motion of a hidden fire
> That trembles in the breast.

This stanza of an old hymn comes to my mind whenever I think of prayer, its solace, its reward, its purpose.

Little folks taught to kneel in humble quietness start aright, for through the stillness that surrounds them all else can be excluded but the recognition of the Great Good that guides, guards, and encourages those who believe.

NOT long ago I was present when a discussion was launched as to the virtue of prayer, of faith, of humbling oneself to an unseen power.

And a wise old philosopher, when asked his view, said, "Why, yes, certainly I believe in the efficacy of prayer, and even if it had no greater power than to quiet one's thought and help one to start anew it would be a wonderful thing." And then he said, "I believe in faith in God as a great principle because it is the safeguard of the human race. If we did not believe in the protecting power of an unseen force, we would not be able to lie down at night and lose consciousness in sleep, for it is chiefly our belief in the safety of our loved ones and ourselves that makes this possible."

And when asked his conception of right prayer, this kindly and wise old man said, "No, I do not believe in supplication, in begging that we may be granted that for which we pray, but I believe in recognizing the power of God to help man face clearly his actual needs and then to express openly an earnest desire for them. To seek good for the sake of good is virtuous, and worthy reverence is always present in sincere prayer, which, even when unspoken, is an expression of faith and kindliness. Such prayers are always answered and more fully than is often anticipated. Learning to eliminate all but the totally essential from one's wishes helps greatly in the sincerity and efficacy of prayer."

AND then he gave examples of sincere worthy desire that were so earnest and so needful that they constituted in themselves most earnest prayer.

Lincoln's Gettysburg address, for instance, which we all know so well. Lincoln's desire to comfort the souls of those who would listen to him on that memorable day was so great that he prayed he might say that which would give peace and assurance to his hearers. When he started on the train to Gettysburg, he had not a word of his speech thought out, but he knew that he must give comfort and in his great sincerity of heart, in his tremendous love for his fellow men, he made the greatest speech in our history. The words came forth from his heart. His hearers were so deeply impressed with the hundred and thirty-four words he spoke that they could not even lift a hand to applaud him.

Each word came as though he were divinely inspired, and surely he must have been to have left grouped together a little handful of words that will inspire, console, and teach men throughout all the years.

Often in our own lives, when we need to advise, comfort, and aid some one, we had best not try to do it until our own sincerity of purpose fairly seethes in our innermost heart. Then what we say will comfort and encourage, what we do will bring peace and just reward, for it will come out of the sincerity of heart, which is in itself the very garden of right prayer.

THIS discussion later turned to the Bible and one man said, "I read the Bible for information, not confirmation. I read to know of the experiences of the human life before us, and the reading encourages me, makes me see beauty and blessedness in today. It makes me more grateful and more tolerant of my own judgment, aims, and desires and those of the people with whom I come in contact."

Where would one find anything more comforting than the twenty-third or the ninety-first Psalm? Where can one find a biography greater than John's story of the life and crucifixion of Jesus? Matthew's version of the Sermon on the Mount inspires and gives peace and consolation to all who earnestly read. We are advised to read Genesis, Exodus, Ruth, Esther, Ecclesiastes, and many other books of the Bible for their purely literary values alone; but to you, my good friends, I bid you read at least our Lord's Prayer in the sixth chapter of Matthew, and sense anew the greatness of the beloved man whose birthday we celebrate at Christmas.

See Him as the good man that He was—kind, patient, tolerant, and true. And then, in the sincerity of your appreciation of Him, create the desire in your heart that you may express more of the love and tolerance and unselfishness that He manifested. Seek this so earnestly that your desire will become a prayer of humbleness and sincerity, and before it is expressed God will have heard and answered you.

I can wish for you nothing greater or more beautiful to make yours a Happy Christmas.

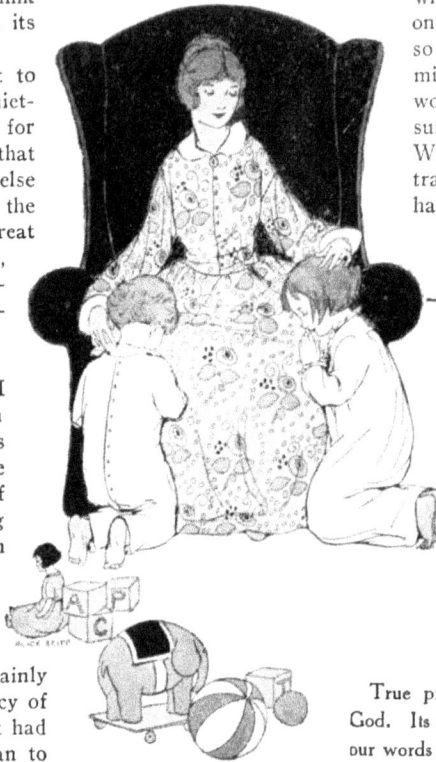

Sometimes a fog will settle over a vessel's deck and yet leave the topmast clear. Then a sailor goes up aloft and gets a lookout which the helmsman on deck cannot get. So prayer sends the soul aloft; lifts it above the clouds in which our selfishness and egotism befog us, and gives us a chance to see which way to steer.

—*Spurgeon*

* * *

True prayer is only another name for the love of God. Its excellence does not consist in the multitude of our words; for our Father knoweth what things we have need of before we ask Him. The true prayer is that of the heart, and the heart prays only for what it desires. To pray, then, is to desire—but to desire what God would have us desire.

—*Fenelon*

* * *

Prayer is the peace of our spirit, the stillness of our thoughts, the evenness of recollection, the seat of meditation, the rest of our cares and the calm of our tempest: prayer is the issue of a quiet mind, of untroubled thoughts; it is the daughter of charity and the sister of meekness.

—*Taylor*

Glittering Hats for Midwinter

By MARY MAHON
Department of Millinery

TRUE to form, after a season of hats of colorless character, Dame Fashion indulges in an extravagantly bright color scheme. With this radical change from the somber all black to the brilliantly bright and vivid colors in millinery for the present winter season, the most distinctive feature is the real elegance of fabrics and trimmings, such as brocades, metal cloth, plumage, rich fruit, flowers that fairly glisten, and all kinds of fur, particularly American broadtail.

Whether this standard of superior merchandise has been advanced by the creators of fashion through their own initiative or the clientele has developed a finer appreciation of quality, is not certain; but regardless of the reason, it is quite refreshing to note that a higher degree of perfection in the matters of dress has been accomplished.

With the use of elegant fabrics, simplicity of effect is the principal requisite for a decidedly modish hat of either large or small dimensions. The windy, blustering days of early winter, together with the style trend of high fur chokers on suits and coats, tend to encourage hats of closer lines and medium off-the-face brims. The Egyptian and Russian lines, with the high-pointed diadem fronts, are unusually flattering, and the wrappy, draped arrangement of the fabric invariably chooses this type of turban for its foundation.

THE smartness of the chic out-of-door turban shown at the upper left of the illustration depends entirely on the artistic arrangement of gorgeous brocade in the new shade of bright blue and silver, with a background of black, which is draped in swatted folds that cross in the front and form the high effect.

This turban is developed on a foundation frame of light-weight netine having a tam-effect top and a slight extension brim that serves to support the soft folds around the face line, its only trimming being two large, ball-shape, iridescent pearl pins thrust through the folds in the front.

FRUITS, especially those which imitate the candied variety, have attained even greater impetus than ornaments as trimming, and their loveliness cannot but be enhanced when they are applied on a medium-size hat suitable for the dance.

The model illustrated at the upper right has a slightly rolling brim at the left side and a medium high crown developed in gold metal cloth. The colorful trim of candied cherries sprayed loosely around the crown and interspersed with dangling loops of metal-edge ribbon continues in a drooping trim at the right side.

In addition to the use of candied fruits, which is a late achievement, there are also numerous flowers of the blossom variety used either in combination with the fruit as wreaths or in small bouquet arrangements. Sometimes a tiny metal or velvet blossom is used as the center of a large petal flower that in many instances is made of fur, brocade, velvet, duvetyn, or any other novelty fabric.

WHILE the vogue of solid fur hats is evident, just now one of the latest and most interesting developments is the combining of fabric and fur, either by covering the entire front of a Russian turban with the fur and making the top of the hat of brocade, metal cloth, or Paisley silks, or by developing the whole hat of the fabric and using the fur sparingly in motifs, or in a strip, as illustrated in the model at the lower right.

This rather pleasing vizor-brim toque is a style that has long been a favorite, and this season finds it just as acceptable in the world of fashion. Pumpkin-shade satin that has been ciréd to look like alligator skin is used to cover the vizor brim and to drape the crown so as to allow for adjustment according to the most becoming angle. A combination wreath of vari-colored blossoms and fruit is applied flat at the base of the crown across the front, and a band of squirrel just above follows the line of the flowers, continuing low around the back. In this model, while brilliant colors are introduced, the blending serves to soften the effect.

DIVIDING honors with the turban as a suitable hat for afternoon wear, we have the long-front, drooping-side backless poke, which has a tendency to roll up at the outer edge, illustrated at the lower left.

The top brim and the crown are made of dark-brown and gold brocade, while a plain, gold metal cloth is used for the under facing, being fitted plain around the outer edge and then drawn into the head-size in fine plaits. The dual side effect, or twin trim, that gained prominence in the early fall season is especially pretty on this model. Matching Chantilly lace is arranged in rosettes, with long cascade ends that hang below the shoulders. Hand-made flowers consisting of four petals developed in brocade and faced with the metal cloth, which is also used to make a small rosebud that forms the center of the flower, are applied in the center of the lace rosettes.

The gracefulness or beauty of this drooping trim is not marred when a large-size fur or wrap is worn, because the frame, being so close to the head, allows the lace to rest on the shoulders on the inside and the collar to be wrapped up over it, thus forming an exceedingly soft outline or frame for the face.

The same shape lends itself wonderfully to an ostrich trim, such as a flat band laid around the crown, with the ends falling off at each side, or, if a touch of fur is desired, to a wreath of hand-made fur flowers appliquéd around the crown. These flowers may be brightened with a center of brilliant glass beads or a tiny metal flower.

ANOTHER thought concerning these tiny hand-made metal flowers is that many of them are constructed out of small scraps of brocade and metal cloth. No corners of fabrics or furs should be discarded this season, because many unique novelties can be worked out with tidbits of tinsel ribbon and material. By combining various kinds of fabrics and colors, designers are transforming into artistic bouquets and ornamental motifs pieces that usually find their way into the scrap bag.

Sweets for the Yuletide Season

By LAURA MacFARLANE
Editorial Department

FOR the good housewife, the Christmas season is a time of increased pleasure. There is something about the spirit of this joyous time that grips her and inspires all her preparations for the happiness of her loved ones. But the making of Christmas sweets is not confined to those experienced in cookery, for it can be enjoyed by even the novice. So, even if you have never done it before, plan to make all your holiday goodies and you will find that you can have just as delicious and attractive ones as those for which your exclusive baker or confectioner asks high prices.

Institute Brownies

A cross between cake and candy is found in Institute brownies, which are most delicious for afternoon teas, evening parties, and similar social affairs.

1 c. sugar	Pinch salt
½ c. butter	½ c. flour
2 eggs	1 c. Eng. walnuts
2 sq. chocolate	½ tsp. vanilla

Cream the sugar and butter, add the eggs beaten very light, and stir in the melted chocolate and salt. Add the flour, chopped nuts, and vanilla. Pour into a square pan and bake 25 minutes. Cut in squares.

Sour-Cream Dainties

A soon as you have some sour cream on hand, try the following recipe. The texture of the cake is so fine and it can be decorated in such charming ways that it makes a much-desired dainty for festive occasions.

2 eggs	1 c. sour cream
1 c. sugar	½ tsp. soda
Pinch salt	1½ c. flour

1 tsp. baking powder

Beat the eggs very light, sift the sugar and salt, and add them; then stir in the cream, to which the soda has been added. Combine the flour and the baking powder, and add to the mixture. Turn into muffin pans of small size, preferably having round bottoms, and bake 20 minutes. When cool, using the rounded bottom for the top, cover with any preferred icing and sprinkle generously with fresh grated coconut. Or, omit the coconut and decorate with nuts or candied fruits.

Sand Tarts

For a small cooky, nothing is nicer than sand tarts. If decorated attractively, they may be used with confections in packing Christmas boxes and baskets. Blanched almonds are the usual decoration, but they may be replaced by English walnut halves, a few chopped nuts, small pieces of candied pineapple, ginger, cherries, or angelica.

½ c. shortening	2 tsp. baking powder
1 c. sugar	¼ tsp. cinnamon
1 egg	1 egg white
1¾ c. flour	Blanched almonds

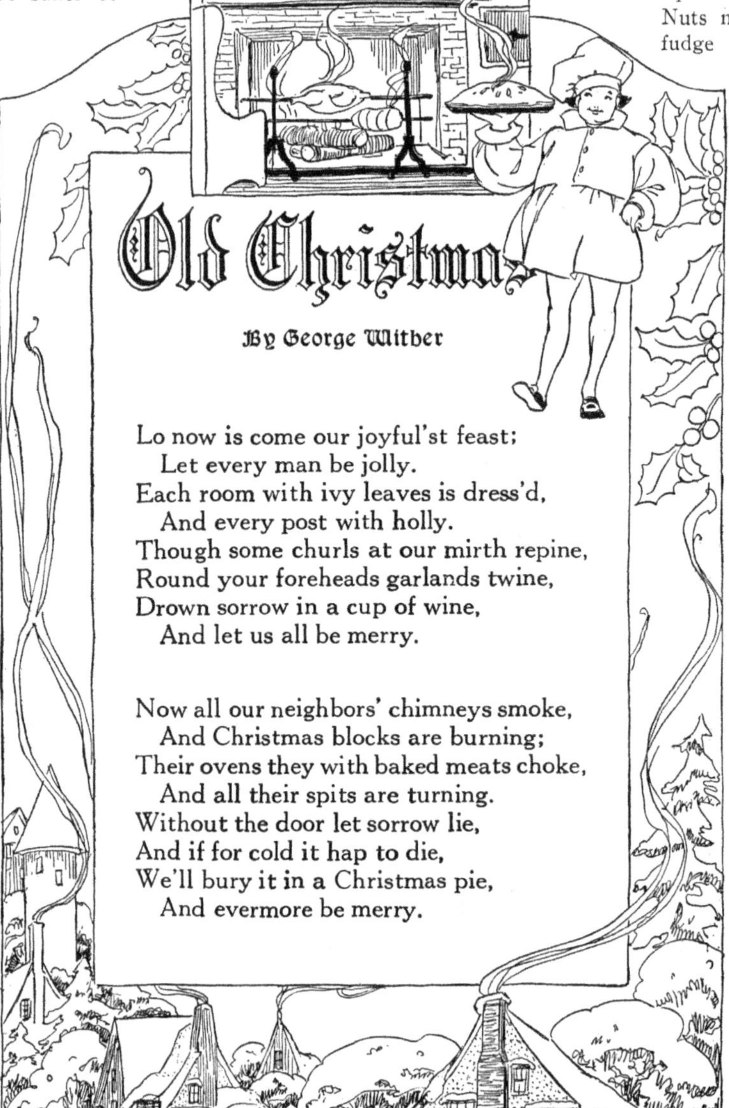

Old Christmas
By George Wither
Lo now is come our joyful'st feast;
Let every man be jolly.
Each room with ivy leaves is dress'd,
And every post with holly.
Though some churls at our mirth repine,
Round your foreheads garlands twine,
Drown sorrow in a cup of wine,
And let us all be merry.
Now all our neighbors' chimneys smoke,
And Christmas blocks are burning;
Their ovens they with baked meats choke,
And all their spits are turning.
Without the door let sorrow lie,
And if for cold it hap to die,
We'll bury it in a Christmas pie,
And evermore be merry.

Cream the shortening and add the sugar and the egg. Sift together the flour, baking powder, and cinnamon, and add to the mixture. Fold in the beaten egg white. Roll very thin, cut, and place on cooky sheet or pan. Decorate with almond halves and bake in quick oven until light brown.

Creamy Fudge

1 Tb. butter	1 tsp. vanilla
2 c. sugar	2 sq. chocolate
¾ c. milk	

Melt the butter, add the sugar and milk, stir well, and boil until a soft ball forms in water or a little on a saucer becomes creamy when worked with a spoon. Add the vanilla and remove from the fire. On a marble slab, a large platter, or a white agate tray, have the grated chocolate and over this pour the hot mixture. Work with a spatula and a knife or two spatulas until the chocolate is thoroughly blended and the mixture becomes creamy. Shape into a square or rectangle and let stand until cool. Cut in squares and remove to a platter or box. Nuts may be added just before the fudge becomes creamy, if desired. Without the chocolate, this makes an excellent vanilla cream candy.

Dropped Fudge

2 c. sugar	2 tsp. butter
1 c. cream	1 tsp. vanilla
2 sq. chocolate	

Stir the sugar and cream and put on to boil. Cut the chocolate into small pieces and add to the mixture as soon as it begins to boil. Cook until a soft ball forms in water, add the butter, remove from the fire, and add the vanilla. Pour into two well-greased soup dishes, dividing the amount equally. Beat that in one dish until it begins to get creamy, and then drop from the spoon onto waxed paper. Beat the other half next and drop in the same way.

Chocolate-Coated Confections

Make up fondant to form a variety of centers, procure small quantities of such nuts as almonds, English walnuts, hazelnuts, Brazil nuts, and pecans, also coat pieces of candied pineapple and candied or maraschino cherries with fondant, and cut up figs and dates into pieces of suitable size. The variety is large, so you may have whatever appeals to you. Put your coating chocolate, which confectioners sell in three varieties—milk, vanilla sweet, and unsweetened—into the upper part of a double boiler and place over boiling water. Set away from the fire until the chocolate starts to melt. Mix, and when the bottom and sides begin to melt, remove from the hot bath and stir slowly. When it registers 85° F., or is melted but not warm, it is ready for use. Drop the centers, nuts, or fruit into the chocolate, one at a time, remove with a fork, and place on waxed paper.

Distributing *Christmas* Cheer

By ALWILDA FELLOWS
Department of Dressmaking

AS a conveyor of the true Christmas spirit, there is no better medium than a handmade gift in which a bit of devotion or friendship and individuality has been secured with each stitch. Fortunately, gifts of such intrinsic value may oftentimes be made at a very trifling or moderate cost, and, thus, there is added satisfaction in their development.

For many of the gifts shown on this page, odds and ends of materials may be used. Any of them will appear well made of very inexpensive materials, provided care and discretion are exercised in the selection.

1. In this camisole of pale mauve Georgette crêpe, pieces cut in triangular fashion and placed at each under arm serve to unite smaller pieces that make up the center-front and center-back portions. The uppermost edges of each of the pieces are finished with double bands of Georgette of a deeper shade of mauve, but even so, the general effect is made very dainty by a band of fine lace, which extends under the points of the camisole.

2. As a means of freshening and modernizing a costume that has already given considerable service, a vest-and-collar-and-cuff set of attractive design is very effective. This dainty set is of sheer batiste with trimming of tucks, feather-stitching, and other fine embroidery and a scalloped needle edge that is unusual. Very narrow lace may be substituted for the needle edge, if desired.

3. Another and a very interesting way of adding an up-to-date note to a costume is by supplying a novelty girdle such as this. Black velvet ribbon forms the two bands at the waist line, the suspended loops and ends, and the greater portion of the rosettes, which are plaited. A row of peacock-blue taffeta ribbon separates the rows of black in the rosettes.

4. This baby's bonnet of organdie is dependent for distinction on the arrangement of its picoted ruffles of self-material. Nevertheless, the tiny roses of chiffon and the fine embroidered sprays that decorate the crown piece are not lacking in effectiveness.

5. Heavy linen in a marquisette weave and of a light ecru covers the square sides of this

bag. A soft, medium shade of green satin forms the lower portion and darker harmonizing green ribbons edge the square sides and form the bands that extend from each upper corner. The appliqué motifs are vari-colored. An interlining of two or more thicknesses of crinoline is required for the sides of the bag.

6. Purses of envelope shape are attracting marked attention at present. This purse interlined with crinoline, lined with satin, and covered with sand-colored duvetyn is of a practical nature because of both its color and its conservative trimming of cross-stitching.

7. The roomy pockets at each end of this crash cover for a child's play table make the putting away of one's toys a simple and enjoyable task rather than an irksome duty. Bindings of deep-orange sateen and appliqué motifs provide a decorative element. A cushion with similar covering would make an excellent companion gift.

8. A prospective bride will be delighted with a pair of pale-blue satin garters such as these, for they will supply that touch of blue which, custom says, is so essential in a trousseau. The addition of pink and mauve chiffon roses in no way detracts from the significance of the blue color note.

9. This negligée of very simple design suggests the use of a great variety of fabrics, for the style is suitable for development in very light-weight fabrics, such as crêpe de Chine, Japanese crêpe, cotton crêpe, or kimono silk, or in materials as heavy as bathrobe fabrics or corduroy. The odd trimming consists of overlapping circles of heavy machine stitching.

10. This trio of handkerchiefs, in which threads of contrasting color take the place of threads of the material which have been drawn out, offers unusual suggestions for decoration. The first boasts squares of contrasting color with tiny rosebuds worked in the bullion stitch, the second a miniature parasol formed of a gathered bit of lace and outlining stitches, and the third a Colonial bouquet, which is made up of French knots of variegated color edged with a ruffle of narrow lace.

11. This lingerie set, consisting of a rosette formed of knotted loops and ends of light-colored ribbon and small gold safety pins concealed by similar loops of ribbon, these pins to take the place of lingerie clasps, has a decided feminine appeal.

12. A square of 1½-inch ribbon forms the foundation for this little sachet bag. The upper edge of this square is turned under, and a small square of sachet is suspended from this edge. The lower edge is gathered and drawn up tightly on the wrong side, thus shaping the bag. The tiny handle is formed of a soft cable cord over which a strip of satin is wound. The tiny roses are of satin also.

13. Ruffles made of narrow ribbon or of picot-edged strips of silk are employed in overlapping rows to cover completely the circular pieces that form the foundation of this unusual bag. Two rows of lace placed at the center of the bag and a row on each side of the opening give a daintiness that is desirable in a light-colored bag, but if dark-colored ribbon is employed, the lace should be omitted.

14. Unbleached muslin is put to many a use nowadays. In this case, it is employed for a very practical carriage or crib cover, but any suggestion of commonness is dispelled by the attractive border of checked gingham and the appliqué motifs that decorate the center. A pillow cover of matching material and design completes the outfit.

15. An idea of the distinction that may be afforded an ordinary cheesebox or a very substantial hat box is evidenced in this workstand of novel design. The cover of the box, which forms the upper shelf, or tray, of the stand, is held in position by substantial pieces of wood, which extend over the main portion of the box and form legs. A stand such as this may be enameled in white or color, or it may be covered with wall paper of appropriate design and lined with mull or similar material.

Woman's Institute *Question Box*

A Correction

In the Fall and Winter issue of Fashion Service we give the address of the Crowell Publishing Company, publishers of the *Woman's Home Companion* and makers of the Woman's Home Companion patterns, as Springfield, Illinois. Please note that this is an error. The address is **Springfield, Ohio.**

"Different" Christmas Cookies

Can you give me some ideas for decorating cookies or other small cakes for Christmas? I have success with my foundation recipes, but I want them to appear "different" this year.
R. D. M.

With just a little effort, you can "dress up" your plain recipes so that you will hardly know them. Cut your cookies with some of the fancy cutters that are in the market, such as hearts, stars, diamonds, animals, etc., and then sprinkle a little coconut or sugar or a few chopped nuts over the top. Or, decorate them with halves of English walnuts, almonds, or pecans, or any desired candied fruit. Nuts may be chopped very fine and added to the mixture before it is rolled out.

Have you ever tried filled cookies? For these, roll the cookies very thin and put two together before baking with a filling of rather stiff jelly, jam, preserves, or conserve. Or, you may make up a special filling by mixing 1 cupful of sugar and 1 tablespoonful of flour, stirring them into ½ cupful of boiling water, adding 1¼ cupfuls of chopped raisins, dates, or figs, cooking until thick, removing from the fire, and then stirring in ¾ cupful of chopped nut meats.

Even doughnuts can be filled. Roll the mixture thinner than usual, cut with a cutter having no hole in the center, brush the edge of one piece with the white of egg, place a teaspoonful of jelly in the center, put another piece on top, and pinch the edge to prevent it from breaking open in the frying. And, instead of making plain doughnuts round in shape, you may vary them by rolling them into long strips and then tying them in a knot or shaping them like a figure 8. Grated orange rind makes a good flavoring for doughnuts.

You can make most attractive little cakes by cutting a rather firm variety, such as pound or fruit cake, into small pieces and then dipping these into melted fondant that has been flavored and colored. A nut meat completes the decoration.

Want to Get Acquainted?

The following Institute students desire to become acquainted with other Institute students residing in their localities:

Fort Wayne, Ind. .... C. E. I.
Seattle, or Kent, Wash. .... E. W.
Hanford, Calif. .... L. B.
Tahlequah, Okla. .... J. A. B.
Mansfield, Galion, and Ashland, Ohio .... E. S.
Willamette Valley, Ore. .... W. P. D.
Richmond, Va. .... S. H.
Roosevelt, Utah .... J. W. A.
Hartford, or Cecil County, Md. .... J. B.
Redmond, Ore. .... B. H.
Detroit, Mich. .... L. M. T.
Canton, N. Y. .... M. M. C.
Bethlehem, Pa. .... E. S.
Brooklyn, N. Y. .... J. D.
Pt. Huron, Mich. .... M. E. D.
Baltimore, Md. .... E. S. B.
San Francisco, Calif. .... O. M. S.
West Chester, Pa. .... M. Z. E.
Philadelphia or York, Pa., or Baltimore, Md. .... F. M. O. M.
Indianapolis, Ind. .... A. E.
Wheatland, Wyo. .... Z. H.
Spuyten Duyvil, New York, N. Y. .... L. M.

I should like to become acquainted with Institute students in the vicinity of Regina, Sask., Canada.
Miss V. Josephine Wright,
General Delivery, Regina, Sask., Canada

I should like to become acquainted with a dressmaker in Allentown, Pa., who would like to have some one help her with plain sewing. A. A. S.

I should like to become acquainted with students or graduates of the Institute who are doing sewing or millinery work in Stockton, or Lodi, Calif. A. F. K.

I should like to correspond with other ministers' wives who are taking the Complete Dressmaking Course. H. B. F.

I should like to become acquainted with Institute students in the vicinity of Marion, Ind.
Mrs. Junabelle Henry,
R. R. No. 5, Marion, Ind.

I should like to correspond with an Institute graduate in Southern Minnesota or Iowa, who has a shop or is going into business and would like an Institute graduate to help her. H. M. W.

I should like to get in touch with other students in Minneapolis, Minn., especially those who are working in specialty shops or conducting establishments of their own. E. M. E.

I should like to correspond with Institute students in the vicinity of Laconia, Ind.
Mrs. Attie A. McKim,
Laconia, Harrison Co., Ind.

I should like to correspond with students about my age, 24 years, who are taking the Complete Dressmaking Course and are interested in starting a dressmaking shop. L. S.

If other Woman's Institute students would like to get in touch with the inquiring students, we shall be glad to supply the addresses that are not printed here.

Our Students' *Own Page*

How I Saved $250 on My Clothes

I have just finished counting up how much I have saved on my clothes since I took up the Woman's Institute Dressmaking Course, and it has been every cent of $250, counting all the hand work on my clothes and at the rate dressmakers charge.

I haven't nearly completed my Course, but have been taking it slowly and enjoying every minute of it. I just finished an unbleached muslin dress with yellow butterflies appliquéd on it, and it took me almost an afternoon to make the butterflies. It cost me just 95 cents, and it is one of the most comfortable and neatest looking dresses I ever had. I have been showered with compliments about it. Now think what a dressmaker would have charged me to make it—at least $8, because I know from experience.

I am taking the Course to do my own sewing, but I have made several dresses for my mother and have just finished two little romper suits for my nephew. I put quite a little hand work on both of them, and I know my sister could not have purchased them for any less than $7 or $8. One of them cost me 58 cents and the other one, the cuter of the two, was made out of some material I had on hand.

So I can't begin to give the Woman's Institute the credit they should have by just telling these few things. I could hardly sew a straight seam when I began this Course—had to have all my clothes, including my plainest undergarments, made. But now I can cut into $4.50 material with just as much confidence as I used to cut into a 10-cent piece of material. This Course has meant at least $500 to me, because the minute I began to study I began to have confidence in myself, and confidence is certainly a big item in sewing. If the women who have not taken advantage of this Course could only understand what it would mean to them, I am sure the Woman's Institute would have all they could take care of and more, too. MRS. CARL CORBIN, Urbana, Ill.

How I Saved $15 a Month on My Groceries

The first year of my married life I felt as if I must aid my husband in some way to add to our income. The only thing I could do was to teach school, so I taught, having to leave my husband to take care of himself and teach also. That year was "terrible," as we were separated by a distance of forty miles. Finally I decided I couldn't stand such a life any longer. Naturally I began to think of means of making money some other way, in order to be nearer home.

In the meantime, while I did housekeeping during the summer, my husband was suffering with indigestion, due, so the physician said, to improperly cooked food. Well, I was almost in despair to think I was the cause of his illness, and we had just about decided, in order to preserve his health, we would have to board. Something just had to happen.

One evening while we were planning what would be best to do, I chanced to notice one of those fascinating stories gotten out by the Woman's Institute, so I decided to try and sent in my name at once. And within a week I was a member of the Institute. I was more interested at first in the cookery, of course, and gave more time to it. I progressed very nicely, indeed, and so did my husband's health. Now I have only three more cookery lessons to study. And I have saved fully $15 per month on our groceries, as I have the record of last year's account, not saying anything about the preservation of my husband's health and possibly my own.

My plan of making money without teaching certainly has proved more profitable than teaching, besides the great saving I have made on my clothes. I have made several hats for my friends and myself at one-third their cost in a store.

My husband joins me in my praises of the Institute. Long live the Institute and may Mrs. Picken's influence live on forever. MRS. BELLE M. CRESWELL, Gatlinburg, Tenn.

How I Saved $135

Last fall I needed a dark-blue tricotine dress in a hurry. It was useless to try to find a dressmaker to make it at once, so I was compelled to look for a ready-made garment. I had studied the Course in Dressmaking and Tailoring only two months, and scarcely felt capable of making such a dress myself. I searched the shops in vain for something that would meet my requirements and my purse. Finally, I saw just what I would want for $78.50. That was more than I could afford for a street dress when I knew that I would also require an afternoon and an evening gown before the season was over.

Almost in desperation, I entered the pattern department and, using the ideas I had acquired while looking at ready-to-wear garments, selected a suitable pattern. Next I purchased 3½ yards of dark-blue tricotine, four skeins of heavy black silk floss, and 2 yards of black moiré ribbon for a sash. In two days I made the dress, and when I wore it the compliments I received gave me courage to try other garments. The knowledge I gained from the lessons on Tissue-Paper Patterns helped me in cutting and fitting properly, which, after all, is one of the most essential things in making smart-looking garments.

My next attempt was a black-velvet afternoon gown and then an evening dress of black dotted net over flesh-colored tissue cloth.

My three dresses cost me exactly $73.92. The tricotine dress could not be purchased for less than $65 and the cheapest velvet dress of the quality of mine was marked at $95. The evening gowns, when priced, proved that the least I would have had to pay was $50. So I saved more than $135 on these three dresses—enough to pay for my Course twice. Then, too, I still had material left to work with when making over.

Since then, the things that I have made over, and the lovely summer dresses I have made for myself and mother, as well as my 3-year-old niece, prove the true value of a knowledge of dressmaking. Now I am working on articles for my trousseau, and I am more than ever thankful for the knowledge gained through the Woman's Institute. MISS MARY M. GOULD, Green Bay, Wis.

How I Saved My Tuition Three Times Over

I have saved the cost of the Dressmaking and Millinery Courses three times over on clothes for myself and my mother, and I now dress better on $150 a year than I did on $275 in 1913, when I went to a very good dressmaker and man tailor.

My principal savings this year have been on a beautiful braided overcoat copied from a model priced at $90, which cost me $20, and I used the very best material, and a cream gabardine suit trimmed with cut openwork, with a taffeta lining and petticoat, and a Georgette blouse. The whole of this cost me $31 and the original was priced at $75. Then I have a navy costume, which looks like a new one and worth $50, but was made at a cost of $15 from a 4-year-old, very faded, green striped suit, which I dyed. I also made a charming evening wrap, which did not cost a cent, as it was made from an old cashmere shawl and some pieces of sable, both of which had been laid away for years as useless.

Besides these things, I have made four lovely hats this year, at a total cost of $6.50 for new material. One of these, a black maline with halo brim and black ostrich crown, is worth $30, and another, a black silk tricorne, with two rose-colored ostrich plumes, looks quite worth $25. I have also made four voile dresses, a serge separate skirt, and two crêpe-de-Chine blouses, and I still have $40 over for shoes, underwear, etc.

My father thought me wildly extravagant when I decided to take the Course, and I often laugh to myself now, when I hear him singing the praises of the Institute to every one. And it is very nice to be able to give my mother pretty things out of my allowance and still to be among the best-dressed people wherever I go. MISS VIOLET TUKE, Cornwall, England

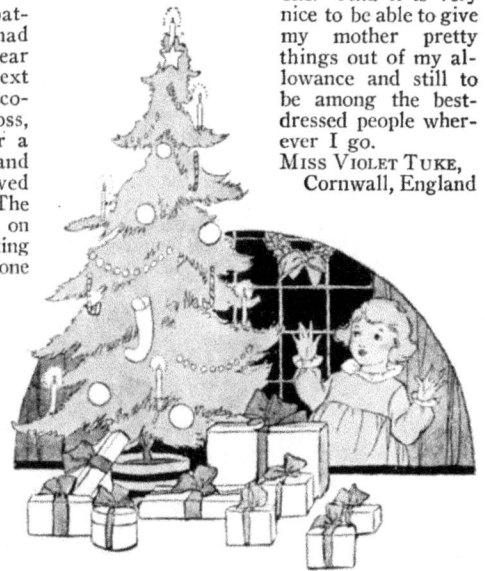

Fashion Service

SUPPLEMENT

Each Issue of *Vintage Notions Monthly* includes a *Fashion Service Supplement*. You will read about the fashion styles popular in the early twentieth century and receive a collectible fashion illustration to print and frame.

The students of the Woman's Institute would also receive a publication called *Fashion Service*. Where the *Inspiration* newsletter instructed them on all aspects of the domestic arts, not only sewing but also cooking, housekeeping, decorating, etc., *Fashion Service* was devoted entirely to giving current fashions with a key to their development.

Fashion Service prided itself on providing it's readers with reliable style information and the newest fashion forecasting. The publication wasn't just eye candy. The Institute stressed the importance of studying the fashions to benefit the sewer's understanding of dressmaking. To quote founder Mary Brooks Picken, "Once the principles of design...and of construction… are understood, beautiful garments will result. This publication comes to you as an aid to this desired goal. Read the text of every page and reason out the why of every illustration and description that your comprehension of designing and construction may be enlarged and your appreciation made more acute."

Today, these articles and illustrations give us a historically accurate view of what fashion really meant 100 years ago. Not only can we study these articles for an "of-the-time" style snapshot, but just as their students did, we can also learn to understand the principles of design and increase our sewing skills. In each issue, look for a collectible illustration in the back of the supplement!

VERSATILITY OF DESIGN MARKS

The softly flared tunic is perhaps the very most important part of Model 8B, a delightfully simple semitailored dress of dark Tyrolian green flat crêpe. The material forms the trimming except for the buttons and the small bow of contrasting velvet ribbon at the neck. The flare of the cuffs is exceptionally smart.

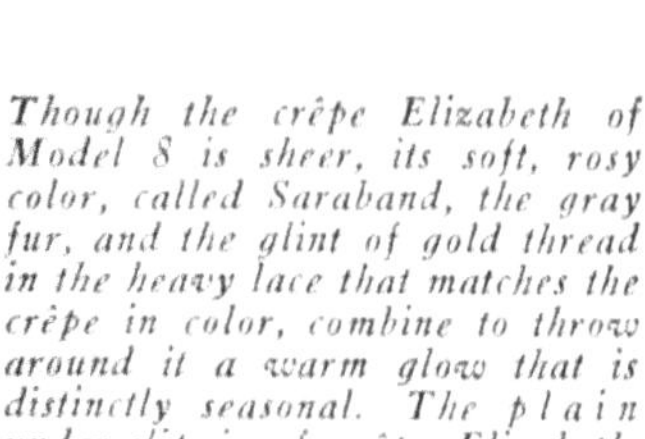

Model 8

8A

8B

Though the crêpe Elizabeth of Model 8 is sheer, its soft, rosy color, called Saraband, the gray fur, and the glint of gold thread in the heavy lace that matches the crêpe in color, combine to throw around it a warm glow that is distinctly seasonal. The plain under-slip is of crêpe Elizabeth.

The black redingote dress, Model 8A, fastened primly from the top of its high collar to the waist line, is unrestrained below, falling open to show its red under-slip, which is revealed again at the bottom of the under-arm seams. Bright embroidered banding enlivens the effect, and godets at the side front give a smart flare.

THE DAYTIME MODE FOR WINTER

The youthful bolero lines of Model 9 are accented by the full-length brocaded chiffon velvet panel in red, white, and black, which contrasts attractively with the black satin of the dress. A slightly molded effect is achieved by means of vertical darts in the back.

A new and much favored fabric combination is plain Georgette and velvet brocaded chiffon. In Model 9A, the joining of the two fabrics follows the design of the brocade. The slightly circular, divided tunic is especially lovely, fluttering as it does with every movement of the wearer. Navy blue Georgette is used with a brocade of brown on a navy ground.

Many points of the mode meet in Model 9B, notable among them being the very new up-in-front, down-in-back line at the hips, the slightly molded bodice, and the flared tunic. Bonnaz embroidery in gold thread contrasts pleasingly with the Moroccan red silk crêpe. Puffed sleeves and vest are of self-material.

THE TREND TOWARD FEMINIZED LINES

Materials and Decorations Are Selected to Accent the Vogue for Grace and Movement

Model 8.—For the foundation over which the long tunic of this model is posed, make a simple costume slip of the dress material. Cut the tunic as you would a straight-line dress, making it 2 or 2½ inches shorter and slashing it up the center front about two-thirds of the way to the low waist line. When you cut the lace for mitering the corners, follow the design, cutting away any parts not needed to fill the space. Very little, if any, more lace is required than for the straight diagonal cut, and the joining is almost invisible. Stitch the lace to the material at the top and cut away the fabric underneath, applying a narrow band of soft fur to the lower edge. Fit the tunic to the hips snugly by several rows of shirring at each side, using long, loose machine stitches and drawing up one thread to produce the gathers.

Model 8A.—The molded lines of this unusual dress require perfect fitting, which makes the development of a muslin model advisable. By doing all fitting in the muslin, it becomes a perfect pattern for the dress. Do not fit this type of dress too closely, for the outlines of the figure must be suggested rather than revealed. Use plain seams for stitching the sections together, pressing the seams open and notching them quite deeply where they curve through the waist-line section, so that they will "set" smoothly. Leave the under-arm seams open below the hip line, turn the seam allowance to the right side, and cover with embroidered banding. Do the same the full length of the center front, and attach the straight, high collar of embroidery. Hook the dress down to the waist line, leaving it unfastened below to show the costume slip beneath.

Model 8B.—The foundation of this model is a straight-line dress with round neck line and fulness gathered on the shoulders. Flares are added by means of the circular tunic, the flared cuffs, and the triangular pieces that form the jabot. The diagram at the right illustrates one half of the pattern used for cutting the front of the graceful tunic.

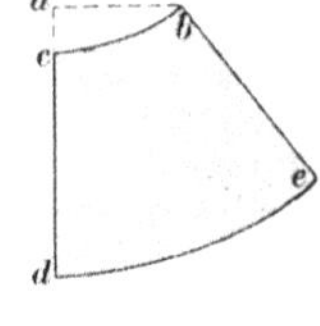

To make the pattern, first measure the distance from the center front of the dress to the side seam at the point where the tunic is to be applied. Then locate point *a* at the upper left corner of a large piece of paper, measuring this distance to the right of *a* and locating *b*. Locate *c* 4 inches below *a* and draw the arc *cb*. On a straight line 20 inches below *c*, locate *d*, drawing the arc *de* parallel with the arc *cb* and twice as long. Draw the straight lines *cd* and *be*. The line *cd* is the center front and is placed on a lengthwise fold for cutting. The back pattern is made in exactly the same way, the only difference being that *ab* is shorter, for it corresponds to the back measurement from center to side seam, which is always somewhat narrower than a similar measurement in front.

Join the two tunic sections, using plain seams, and bind the lower edge with self-material. Apply the tunic to the dress, turning it upward against the dress with its wrong side out so that the stitching will not show on the right side after it is turned back in position. Bind the straight edges of the jabot, apply the bias edges to the dress, and cover the joining with a double band of material that extends to the bottom of the tunic, slip-stitching this band in place. Cut the cuffs circular, finish them double, and apply them 3 inches from the wrist.

Model 9.—This skilfully cut dress in bolero effect introduces a full-length under-front of brocaded velvet that is joined to the dress itself in the shoulder and under-arm seams. Turn back deep hems on the front-skirt sections of satin to reveal a wide panel of the brocade. The top of each of these sections is attached to the wide belt, which is cut in one with the bolero sections. Make a 10-inch slashed-and-bound opening in the top of the velvet panel. Face the edges of the bolero and the belt. Line the collar with satin and attach it to the dress. To fit the dress snugly over the hips, make an inturned tuck at each side of the back, as shown.

Model 9A.—It is the clever use of material in this modish model that "makes" the dress. If you can secure 54-inch material with velvet brocade running through the center, your work is simplified. If not, the effect is easily obtained by inserting brocade between two strips of plain Georgette before cutting the straight-line dress. Cut the four draperies slightly circular, following the general method described for the tunic of Model 8B. In this case, however, have your line *ac* 2 inches long and *cd* about 17 inches long. Make *de* a little less than twice as long as *cb*. Bind the edges and attach the four draperies to the dress at the bottom of the brocaded section, stitching them as suggested for the tunic of Model 8B.

Model 9B.—The under dress of this smart model is made with a full-length front of the dress material and a back of lining silk with a deep band of the dress material at the bottom. Sleeves that are full at the bottom may be sewed into this under dress, or short puffs may be tacked to the sleeves of the overdress, as preferred. Cut the blouse section of the overdress like a plain dress, making it long enough to allow for attaching the circular tunic. Slash it down the center front and turn back and face the edges for revers. Be guided by the pattern in cutting the front-tunic sections, and cut the back tunic as described for Model 8B. Draw the material into soft folds in attaching the buckles.

YOUTHFUL MODES FOR EVERY NEED

Model 10.—A holiday party becomes an especially happy occasion when it can be enjoyed in a frock like this. A youthful face will glow like a flower above white Georgette and pale green ribbon bows, provided the coloring of hair and skin is light; if not, yellow Georgette with gold-color velvet ribbon will prove more becoming.

First cut a simple straight-line dress. Then cut the apron, making it straight at the top and curving the lower edge up toward the center back. Allow plenty of fulness to provide the proper setting for the bows that are placed quite regularly on its surface. Finish the edges of the apron with machine picoting and bind the neck edge and armholes with a narrow bias of self-material. A butterfly bow of the Georgette with shaped ends brought up to the shoulders and tacked in place, is an interesting variation in waist-line finishes.

Model 10A.—Navy blue balbriggan with trimming stitches of wool floss in shades of magenta, corn-flower blue, and medium green satisfies mother because it will wear well, and daughter because it is colorful and smart. The embroidery, which should be done before the collar is attached, consists of two rows of simple darning-stitches and one row of rather large cross-stitches. Round the collar and finish its edge with cross-stitches taken directly over a tiny hem.

Bind the neck opening and finish it with loops and self-covered buttons, over which work cross-stitches in the wool used for the embroidery.

Model 10B.—The slot seam and the circular skirt are two smart details of Fashion, and when both are combined in one dress, its wearer may be assured of being delightfully in the mode. Cocoa-brown rep is the material used, with collar and cuffs of écru linen and a dark brown tie. Before cutting, plan the position of the slot seams; then baste them, arranging the opening in the one at the left. Finish the neck line and lower edges of the sleeves completely and the collar and cuffs separately, making these of a double thickness or of a single thickness with the edges bound, and sewing them on by hand so that they may be removed readily for cleaning.

Because of the tailored effect of this little dress, it is essential that each detail be carefully carried out, especially the basting, stitching, and pressing. Attention given to these points makes not only a better-looking dress but a better-wearing one, too.

Model 10C.—Repeating in the cape the shape of the applied circular skirt sections of this dress produces a costume that is both practical and smart. In this instance, dark green faille uses a narrow strip of beaver for a collar and adds dainty lingerie cuffs, with the result a "best" dress thoroughly suited to the many informal social activities of its youthful wearer.

A slash, deep enough to allow of ease in putting on and taking off, is concealed under the beaver-colored ribbon bow that finishes the center front. If desired, the cape may be lined with a light-weight silk crêpe that will match the fur in color, or its edges may be finished with a narrow self-binding, this finish being repeated on the circular skirt sections.

If the cape should seem a little bulky for wear under a coat, it can be finished separately, then attached with small hooks and eyes so it may be removed readily. To be as inconspicuous as possible when the cape is not being worn, the eyes should be of silk floss of a color that matches the dress exactly.

FASHION'S OFFERINGS TO

Ruffles and rosebuds and circular flounce conjure up a dainty picture when associated with a child's party dress. The picture becomes concrete in Model 11, with body and rose trimming of tea-rose Georgette and flounce and yoke of matching taffeta.

Plaid taffeta, crisp and colorful, is ideal for Model 11B with its perky bias godets. Red bows on the hips repeat the predominant color of the plaid. Worn with a tam and a taffeta-lined coat of black velveteen, it would effect a distinctive ensemble.

The wee lass who wears Model 11A, might have come from the Scotch highlands yesterday, so much of the very air of them clings to her gay plaid plaited skirt and black velveteen blouse. Collar and cuffs are of white linen.

Pink crêpe de Chine is in itself the very embodiment of girlish daintiness. Add to it grosgrain ribbons of a slightly deeper tone that are set a-flutter by the slightest movement, and you have Model 11D, a dress to make merry eyes dance with joy.

Red embroidered dots, one to each frill-edged scallop, give a unique touch to Model 11C. Navy peau de soie, a fine twilled material, makes the dress, and red crêpe de Chine, the collar, cuffs, and frills. The fulness supplied by the inverted plait at the center back is confined by the belt.

The revival of patch work may or may not have inspired the puff sleeves of Model 11E, made by sewing together strips of orange, green, and brown crêpe de Chine. The dress is coffee brown and the roses at the belt ends are of orange and yellow fabric with green leaves.

(For detailed instructions, see Page 34)

THE SMART JUNIOR MODE

For the girl who is beginning to appreciate the dignity of "grown-uppish" fashion points in her own frocks, there is Model 11I of Alpine green crêpe faille. The front and back skirt fulness, shaped bands, and heavy lace collar, all have their appeal.

The coziest and gayest of schoolroom frocks is made from wool challis, as shown in Model 11J. The simple lines of the dress are well chosen, for they show the colorful design to advantage. Trimmings are of plain challis in a harmonizing color.

The quaint charm of a wine-and-cream English print is enhanced by touches of black embroidery in Model 11H. Crenelated lines of running-stitches border the skirt, and tiny black rambler roses are sprinkled generously over the front.

The question of how and how much to trim a child's dress, though often a puzzling one, is charmingly answered by the hand-made grapes, ruffles, and broad hem band of Model 11G, all in turquoise blue. The dress is of white crêpe de Chine.

That the small boy keeps tabs on fashion is proved by Model 11K, of blue chambray with white lawn pin-tucked vestee in bosom effect. The buttoned tab is both useful and ornamental.

Following faithfully the grown-up mode, Model 11F, with its long tunic of black kasha, is worn over a knife-plaited skirt of black-and-yellow striped flannel. The same striped flannel makes the lower sleeves, and black grosgrain ribbon binds all edges and effects the closing by means of tiny bows.

No young gentleman objects to hand embroidery on his clothes provided it is done in a thoroughly masculine way, as on Model 11L. In this case, the natural pongee blouse is embroidered with brown arrowheads and running-stitches, matching in color the heavy wool jersey trousers and silk tie.

(For detailed instructions, see Page 34)

YOUTH IN FASHION'S SPOTLIGHT

Simple Lines Accented by Interesting Trimmings Characterize the Youthful Wardrobe

Model 11.—Join the front and the back pieces of this dress to the yoke and join the circular flounce sections to these. Then make the under-arm seams as for a kimono-sleeve dress. The single taffeta ruffles that edge the yoke are inserted in the plain seams. Double ruffles, gathered through the center, cover the joining of the flounce to the dress.

Model 11A.—Outline the low waist line on a straight-line, one-piece pattern and use the upper part for cutting the velveteen blouse of this model. Sew up the blouse and gather the slight fulness at the bottom. Prepare the straight, knife-plaited skirt and join it to the blouse with a narrow belt. Cover the front opening of the blouse with a band of the plaid.

Model 11B.—In developing this dress, cut the godets bias, insert them with plain seams, and then sew up the under-arm seams. Bind the sleeve edge, and continue the binding along the shoulder seams of the front section. Lap this over the back and sew up the shoulder by stitching on the crease of the binding. Gather the slight fulness at the front and bind the neck line.

Model 11C.—Pin or baste the center-back inverted plait in the material before cutting this dress if a pattern with a plain back is used. The plait is stitched only at the neck line. The method of applying the plaited frills to the scallops is illustrated and explained on Page 44. Embroider the dots before applying the scallops so that the facing will cover them on the wrong side.

Model 11D.—Cut the waist of this dress so that it is very little longer than the lining, for it should blouse only slightly. Join the bottom of the blouse and the top of the skirt to the bottom of the lining. Tack the loops of ribbon to the skirt so that each one overlaps the one beneath it slightly, letting the ends hang free. Tack the ribbon to the blouse by the inner edge only.

Model 11E.—Bind the edge of the front overskirt of this model with orange silk, and apply a fold of the same width of green silk just above it. Then gather the fulness in the overskirt section, and, in sewing it to the straight edge of the blouse, include in the seam the under front, which extends up to the waist line. Leave the top edge of the under front unattached between the two groups of gathers. Seam the under arms without including the overskirt edges.

Model 11F.—Cut the tunic blouse as you would a plain dress, but from 5 to 6 inches shorter. Bind the bottom, the opening slash, and the neck line with grosgrain ribbon. Tack ribbons 7 inches long to opposite sides of the opening for each bow fastening, finishing the lower-sleeve sections in the same way. Attach the plaited skirt to an under-waist.

Model 11G.—Cut the white part of this dress 1¾ inches shorter than the dress is to be when finished. Shirr and insert the godets in the front. Then cut straight bands of the blue crêpe 4½ inches wide for the double band at the bottom, which is 2 inches wide when finished, and apply as any binding. Make the fabric decorations as described and illustrated on Page 44. The neck and sleeves are finished with tiny ruffles and binding.

Model 11H.—Finish the neck of this plain little bloomer dress with a double collar of lawn, the sleeves with a narrow band of self-material, and the bottom with a 2-inch hem. Measure the width of the skirt and block out with pins the lines for the running-stitch border. The lower line comes at the top of the hem. Make the rambler roses 2½ to 3 inches apart.

Model 11I.—The slight fulness in the blouse of this dress is provided by cutting the under-arm line so that it slants slightly away from the pattern toward the bottom. Join the shoulder and under-arm seams of the blouse and the side seams of the skirt. Gather all skirt fulness in little groups at the center front and center back, and keep the under-arm seams of blouse and skirt together when joining them. Arrange an opening under the front band.

Model 11J.—The opening of this dress is on the left shoulder and continues on down the line of trimming 4 or 5 inches, as indicated by the buttons. The neck line is cut quite high and the collar pattern is worked out in muslin. From the shoulder opening to the center front, the collar is finished separately and held by snaps.

Model 11K.—Pin-tuck the material and make the center box plait before cutting the deep U-shaped vest of this tiny suit. Make the little tab double and turn it with seams inside. Stitch the vest to the waist along the curved line, catching the tab in the seam at the bottom of the plait. Join the shoulder and under-arm seams, attach the collar, and insert the sleeves. Make a buttonhole in the tab and sew a button to the trousers.

Model 11L.—In this suit, the panel in the blouse front, with its three rows of running-stitches, each ending in an arrowhead, is cut wide enough to have the edges turned under in ½-inch plaits. The opening is under the right-hand plait. Stitch the plaits first on the machine and then make running-stitches over the machine-stitching.

NEW DEVELOPMENTS IN HOME FROCKS

Featuring Fabrics and Lines That Are New to the Kitchen, and Novelties in Gift Aprons

Model 12.—House dresses have evolved from the bungalow apron stage to one of distinct individuality. Some of the newest style features are to be found flitting briskly between sink and range! There is, for example, this dress with its modish flare. Since skirt fulness is a necessity in the perfect house dress, it is evident that the choice is a happy one. The fulness in this case is provided by the circular cut of the skirt, so that there are the same number of seams as in a straight-line dress. Use plain, overcasted seams, fitting the dress in a little through the hips and waist. Make the front opening band of self-material, fastening it with buttons and buttonholes. The collar and cuffs are double, either two thicknesses of the print, or with a lining of lawn.

Model 12A.—The smock as an item of kitchen wear is a rather new idea, but a decidedly good one. Not only is it entirely practical for this new rôle, but it helps to establish the household arts on the high plane where they belong.

A dress or long overblouse pattern may be used for the smock. Choose one that has fulness allowed in front. Then across the back, outline the straight yoke 4 inches below the center-back neck line. Cut the pattern on this line and use the upper part as the yoke pattern, allowing a ⅜-inch seam on the lower edge.

Provide fulness in the lower back section by laying the center back of the pattern about 2½ or 3 inches from the lengthwise fold of the material. Cut along all pattern edges except the center back, and allow ¾ inch for the seam at the top. At the center front, provide enough width for a 1-inch hem on each side. A smock is always cut a little shorter than the dress.

Cut the sleeves rather wide toward the bottom and slash a 3-inch opening at the bottom of each so that they may be rolled up, if desired. Finish these slashes with narrow bindings or tiny hems. Then when the sleeves are stitched up, gather the bottom and apply the cuff bands, making them long enough to overlap and button.

The lapel facing, collar, cuff bands, and pockets are of plain-colored Everfast.

Model 12B.—Comfortable width is provided in the skirt of this dress by means of the inverted center-front plait, a straight inset of material being used in this plait. The first thing to do after the dress is cut out is to sew the inset to the two front sections, using plain, overcasted seams. Then lay the inverted plait, making it deep enough so that the vest just fits the cut-out section in the dress front. Baste the plait carefully in place. Then bind the outer edges of the vest and lay it on the dress front so that its edges overlap the cut-out section, basting it in position and stitching at the edge of the binding. With this completed, apply the lapel facing. The whole front is now complete and ready to be stitched at the shoulders and armholes to the front edges of the epaulet sleeves.

Next, stitch the back of the dress to the back edges of the sleeves, and sew up the under-arm seams of dress and sleeves in one as you would those of a kimono-sleeve model. Apply the collar and cuffs and hem the skirt. The pockets may be real or simulated.

Model 12C.—Haven't you often wished that you had some attractive means of keeping a pot holder close at hand for instant use? Here, then, is your solution of the difficulty. At first glance, the tea things appear to be substantially applied trimmings of cretonne. But a glance at the detail below on this page will show you that the teapot is a pot holder, padded well with cotton, quilted, and bound with bias tape. It buttons to the little outlined skeleton of itself on the apron by means of a bias-tape loop. The sugar bowl is similarly bound, but has no need of padding and quilting, for it is a pocket. As for the apron itself, it is made of a square of unbleached muslin with the upper corner cut off and the edges bound. Little tucks at the waist line take in superfluous fulness. Tiny safety pins, sewed to the upper corners, fasten it to the dress.

Model 12D.—To make a pattern for this tiny apron, start with a square of paper. Cut a small square from one corner, making the two points of the bib, and round off the other three corners.

Finish the edges of the apron with embroidery edging, put on with tiny flat-felled seams or with machine hemstitching. Shirr the fulness over the hips, and cover with ribbon bows and tie.

Model 12E.—Both the apron itself and the bib are cut with straight side edges, the apparent shaping being done by gathering the fulness at the waist line. Shape the lower edge by cutting it in three points of equal width and depth. Insert the lace, stitching the edges to the material, cutting the material out from under it, and turning back the edges as tiny hems or as rolled hems.

Some morning, when a gingham house dress seems just a bit unfriendly, try slipping into a cozy little frock of wool challis. This delightful material is made in attractive stripe designs that work up in such trim effects as Model 12B. The bindings are of harmonizing bias tape or plain challis.

The teapot that is quickly unbuttoned and removed to become a pot holder is the novel feature of Model 12C. The cretonne sugar bowl is stitched securely to this unbleached muslin apron.

FASHION TURNS KITCHENWARD

Flares have found their way into the kitchen! It is only right that they should, for one could not imagine a more comfortable dress for the morning's duties than Model 12 with its generous skirt width. It is made in your favorite color of sateen with trimmings of English print.

Another newcomer in the kitchen is the smock, or the kitchen coat, as some women prefer to call it. A picturesque cretonne version of this garment is shown in Model 12A. It is practical, for it slips on easily like a coat, enveloping and protecting the frock. And it is so good looking!

A tea apron that is worn becomingly by any one, from grandmother to her debutante granddaughter, is Model 12D, of white dimity with fine embroidery edging.

The daintiest of the new tea aprons are of organdie in white or pastel colors. Model 12E, with its inserts of lace, is well adapted to this crisp fabric.

(For detailed instructions, see Page 35)

With the jabot for grace and the Gypsy girdle for smartness, Model 13A would draw favorable attention without the additional interest given by the bordered printed crêpe de Chine of which it is fashioned. Plain material, matching the background of the print in color, is used for the collar and jabot, which are edged with the narrow band that is found on the unbordered edge of the newest 54-inch bordered materials. The epaulet shoulder gives the desired slim shoulder line.

STYLES THAT MIGRATE SOUTH

Characteristic of the kasha sports frock is Model 13B of natural grege color with bands of red crêpe de Chine. Width is supplied and smartness accented by the box plaits at the side fronts.

A surprising combination that is popular for southern wear is the skirt of pink kasha with white broadcloth overblouse, seen in Model 13C. For northern wear, the skirt would be of tan.

By means of its smocked yoke, Model 13 varies the usual masculine lines of the popular jumper dress. Pastel colors are employed in such a frock for southern wear. This model is charming in warm wine-red for immediate wear in the north.

(For detailed instructions, see Page 38)

SOUTHERN STYLES PREDICT SPRING MODES

With Pastel and Crayon Tints at the Winter Resorts, Spring Bids Fair to be a Season of Flower Coloring

Whether or not one is planning to spend the season at one of the southern resorts, it is interesting to know what will be worn there. For a peep at southern wear is just like lifting the lid of Fashion's box of spring plans, because the things that will be worn a little later when spring really comes to the north, are influenced profoundly by the lines, the colors, and the fabrics that are favored at Palm Beach and other resorts now. And some of them may be adapted for immediate northern wear.

So, while Dame Fashion is in a mood to take us into her confidence, let us see a few of her advance offerings.

Model 13.—The two-piece dress continues in the forefront of popularity. Here we have a raglan-sleeve model with soft fulness shirred, or smocked, to a becoming yoke line in the back and over the shoulders, while the front remains plain. To preserve this plainness in front, narrow the front-pattern piece before cutting the material. To do this, hold the pattern up to the figure so that the under-arm and shoulder lines are in the proper location. Then fold the pattern over at the center line of the figure, thus taking out the surplus fulness. Lay this pattern fold on a lengthwise fold of material for cutting the dress.

The back may be cut in one piece, or in two if the material cuts to better advantage that way, for the applied band at the center back will cover the seam. The opening is by means of a bound slash at the center front.

Sew the front and the back to the raglan sleeves with plain seams. Before sewing up the under-arm seams, shirr, or smock, the yoke fulness, fitting it to the figure as you work. Then make the under-arm seams as for a kimono-sleeve model. Make the band at the center back as you would a belt, and let the stitches that hold the buttons secure this also. Fit the blouse smoothly over the hips.

The skirt is cut in two pieces with slightly gored seams on the hips. Arrange three box plaits in the front, and gather any slight fulness over the hips and center back when the skirt is attached to the camisole lining.

Model 13A.—Some truly artistic bordered silks in 54-inch widths are offered in the shops. The newest of these have narrow bands of solid color along the unbordered edge, providing for trimming bands for collar and cuffs.

For this model, use a plain epaulet-shoulder foundation and cut the deep V line that extends from the inner ends of the shoulders to the low waist line. Over this drape the jabot collar in muslin. Start with a straight piece of muslin, like a convertible collar across the back, having it as long as the narrow border shown. Pin the center of this to the back-neck line and leave the ends loose. Use triangular pieces for the jabot drapes, attaching the bias edges to the V-neck line and pinning the straight tops of these to the ends of the long collar. Remove the muslin from the dress, having the jabots still pinned to the collar, and use it as a pattern, cutting the two jabots and collar in one, or arranging a seam at the center back of the collar.

The Gypsy girdle is just a straight piece of the material about 8 inches wide. Use a strip cut across the full width of the material, and, to the unbordered end of this, attach a strip 20 inches long, cut from the bordered edge. When the girdle is tied as shown, one end loops over the piecing seam and conceals it.

Model 13B.—Sports frocks are leading all others for southern wear, and in these the combination of kasha with crêpe de Chine is most popular. The fulness is invariably supplied by plaits.

This dress is made on straight lines with two applied box plaits at each side of the front. Apply the straight bands of colored crêpe de Chine that extend from the bust line to the points where the tops of the plaits will come, stitching very close to the turned-in edges. To mark the position of the plaits, run a row of long basting-stitches from the lower end of each band to the bottom of the dress. Prepare each box plait by folding under the edges so that they meet at the center on the wrong side, and by shaping the upper end to a point, cutting off the point of the under thickness.

To each side of the row of basting-stitches, apply one of the box plaits, having their edges touch over the bastings. Turn under the edges of the pointed ends about ¼ inch and slip-stitch to the dress. Slash the dress under the center line of each of these box plaits, and cut away the rectangle of material between these two slashes. Sew the outer edge of each plait to the slashed edge of the skirt beneath it, and fill in the space where the skirt material was removed with a straight piece of contrasting material, sewing the edges of this to the loose edges of the box plaits.

Model 13C.—The unusual feature of this blouse is the method of disposing of the fulness. The trim, closely-fitted hip line so necessary in the smart silhouette is attained by making four small inverted plaits across the front and stitching them for a depth of some 5 or 6 inches. Shoulder and wrist fulness is disposed of in tiny inturned tucks, which give practically the same effect as the inverted plaits.

The circular skirt is cut in two pieces, with seams on the hips. It may be sewed to a camisole lining, although the newest skirts are using very narrow stay belts at the normal waist line. If this finish is used, arrange a placket at the top of the left-side seam. Let the skirt hang two or three days before finishing the bottom. Then face it with bias strips of self-material.

IN THE REALM OF WINTER SPORTS

Sports Attire Is Chosen for Freedom of Movement, Comforting Warmth, and Colorful Appeal

Model 14.—The jersey of which this costume is made comes in tube form, which simplifies the making of the skirt. Since the total width, or circumference, of the tubing is 54 inches, a comfortable short-skirt width, one needs only to cut off a skirt length of material, hem it, and attach it to a camisole, taking in the fulness at the hips with darts or gathers. Made in this way, the skirt has no side seams.

Before cutting the turtle-neck blouse, cut the jersey tube open along one fold, when it will appear as any 54-inch material, folded double.

The seams of jersey garments are peculiarly prone to rip. To prevent this, stitch all seams twice, having the two rows of stitching very close together. Use a slightly loose tension because the jersey is somewhat elastic. Overcast all seams closely.

The collar may be lined with crêpe de Chine if one objects to wool so close about the neck. Use wool yarn in bright colors for the embroidery, being careful to blend them well, both with each other and with the background of jersey. Simple stitches should be used, the blanket-stitch and chain-stitch being most successful because they are just as elastic as the jersey.

Model 14A.—To give the greatest possible protection, the wind breaker is lined with wool jersey. Cut the lining exactly like the outside and join the parts with plain seams, stitched twice with a rather long stitch and loose tension. Use flat-felled seams throughout for the outer part. Stitch the pockets to the jacket before lining it.

Place the front edges of jacket and lining together with right sides together and stitch close to the edge on both right and left sides. Turn so that the wrong sides come together, and stitch on the outside about 1/4 inch from the edge to conform with the appearance of the flat-felled seams. Turn the jacket wrong side out with the lining over it, wrong sides still together, and tack the two together at the shoulder and under-arm seams, and at the armholes.

For the knitted bands, use wool yarn of medium weight and small needles so that the bands will be tightly knitted and firm. You will want the ribs of knitting to run at right angles to the point of attachment, so for the neck band measure the number of inches around the neck opening, casting on enough stitches to give this length. Then knit two, purl two, knit two, and purl two, continuing thus across the entire width. On the second row, purl two and knit two, so that the purling comes where the knitting did on the opposite side, thus forming the wide ribs. If you prefer narrow ribs, knit one and purl one, reversing the stitches on the second row. Continue knitting and purling until you have a band twice as wide as the finished collar is to be. Cast off the stitches and apply the collar double to the neck line. Make the wrist and hip bands in the same way, first measuring to get the length correct. Many of these knitted bands are worked out in novelty stitches and Indian designs by using bright colors. If you are an experienced knitter, you may enjoy working out an original band design.

Plain seams with notched edges are used for the knickers. The side seams are left open about 7 inches at the top and finished with plackets which fasten with bone buttons. Leave the lower ends of the side seams open 2 inches and finish with facings, or by merely hemming the edges back, thus providing the openings that are necessary with knickers that fasten with tight bands below the knee. The bands are interlined with percaline.

Model 14B.—A short coat of this type is made in the same general way as is a large, full-length coat, the instruction on Page 27 being applicable to it. A light interlining of one thickness of cotton flannel is advisable.

Notice that the stitching is very prominent, being used as a trimming feature. For this reason, it must be as perfect as possible, with stitches rather long.

The skirt is gored very slightly, cut in three pieces, and made with insets in the plaits. Use plain seams in inserting the insets, having the seams come in the folds of the plaits. Gather the small amount of fulness at the top and sew the skirt to a camisole or finish it with a belt.

Model 14C.—To cut the blouse of this garment to the best advantage, cut the jersey tubing open along one fold so that it may be folded in any way that is necessary. Stitch the shoulder, under-arm, and sleeve seams twice because of the tendency of seams in jersey garments to rip. These are plain seams, overcasted closely. Make the collar, cuffs, front-opening band, and hip band of the tweed. Line the collar with silk because tweed is somewhat rough and is likely to irritate the skin. Work buttonholes in the front opening band and collar, and sew bone buttons to the other side of the opening.

The skirt is cut in two pieces, the front one much wider than the back, with slight goring on the hip seams. Bring the fulness of the front over to the left side and arrange it in four knife plaits. In order that the skirt may fit well all around, gather in a small amount of fulness on the right hip, and a little more across the back. This will not show below the hip line, above which it is entirely covered by the jumper.

Prepare a camisole top and join the skirt to it with a felled seam. Some prefer camisoles that may be removed for cleaning. Such a camisole is finished at the bottom as a separate garment, the skirt is put on a narrow belt, and the two are attached by means of very large snap fasteners, sewed close together.

METALLIC FABRICS AND SLASHED BRIMS

Early predictions of more elaborate millinery for winter wear are being borne out in every detail of fabric and trimming. Winter hats are large, graceful, well-trimmed, and decidedly ornate with the glitter of jewels and of gold, copper, and silver brocade.

Designed to complete a smart afternoon or dress-up costume, the model shown in side view on this page and in front view on the next page stresses these new features. The brim, with its side slashes permitting the wreath of flowers to continue through to the under facing, shows a tendency to assume the task of trimming as well as to help balance the flared skirt of the present mode.

The slashed-brim effect, introduced this season, does not mean just cutting a slash in a regulation brim; rather, the brim is made in sections and the slashes are fitted together, thereby making a pliable and substantial fabric brim, such as is shown here.

Developing the Brim Pattern.—To develop the pattern of this two-section brim, lay a piece of tissue paper over Fig. 1, which is one-half of the back pattern, and trace its outline; then trace the outline of Fig. 2, or one-half of the front section. After obtaining a perfect outline of these two figures, marking and lettering them as indicated, cut around the outline.

For the back-section pattern, fold a large sheet of tissue paper and lay Fig. 1 with the end *ab*, or center back, on the fold of the paper, and pin secure; then cut along the line *bc*, or the outer edge, and the curved line *cde*, or the side slash. Trace the curve *ae* for the inside head-size line. Next, continue line *ab* and curve *cde* ¾ inch and indicate a new line everywhere ¾ inch from the line *ae*, to allow for tabs around the head-size band. A pattern of one-half the brim, or the back section, will then appear as in Fig. 3.

For the front-section pattern, pin Fig. 2 with the line *ab* on the fold of the paper, cut along the lines *bc* and *cde*, and trace curve *ae*; then allow the ¾-inch margin beyond the line *ae* as for the back section, and the pattern of the front section appears as in Fig. 4.

Lay these patterns on a piece of netine with the lines *ab* on the straight of the material and cut around the outer edges. Then, slash the tabs to the head-size line. Before joining these two sections together, bind the edge of the side slashes, as at *cde* on both sections, with a bias of crinoline. Then lap these sections, as shown at *a*, Fig. 5, making the lap ½-inch wide, and pin secure. Next, attach the edge wire, as shown at *b*. Also, apply a ribbon-wire head-size band.

Making the Hat.—To cover the brim, lay the pattern on the fabric as directed for the frame and cut, allowing ¾ inch around the outer edge and sides for turning over the edges. Lay the cut fabric over the front section of the top brim, stitch secure around the head-size, and then turn it over the outer edge. At the joining on the sides, make a

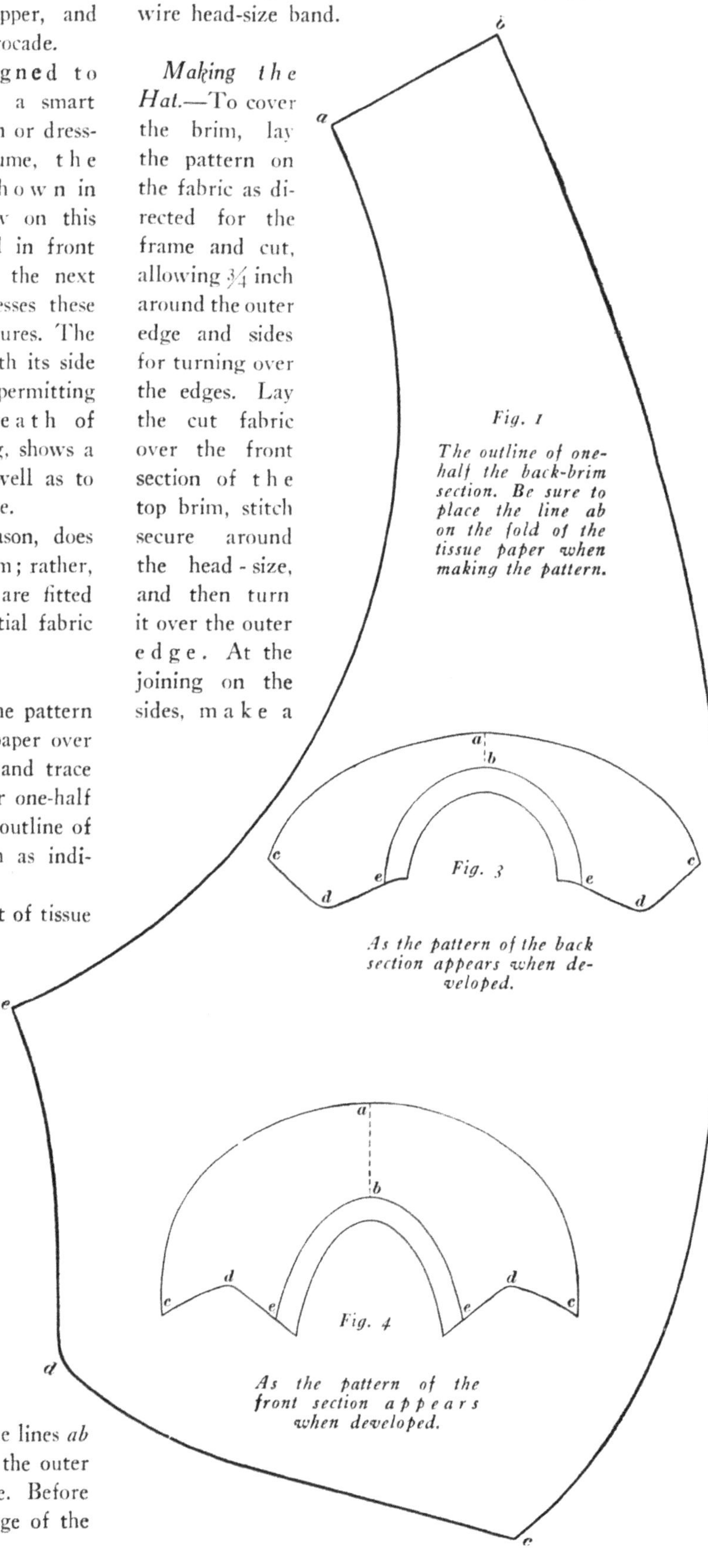

Fig. 1

The outline of one-half the back-brim section. Be sure to place the line ab on the fold of the tissue paper when making the pattern.

Fig. 3

As the pattern of the back section appears when developed.

Fig. 4

As the pattern of the front section appears when developed.

CHARACTERIZE WINTERTIME MILLINERY

tiny slash in the material just inside the edge and work it neatly over the wire and over the edge of the slash. Cover the back section in the same way, but at the side slash turn the material over the edge for a finish, as at *a*, Fig. 6.

Before attaching the under facing, apply the maline transparent extension flange around the outer edge. To make this flange, double 1¼ yards of maline over a 46-inch steel wire. Run a shirr string along the raw edges, draw it up tight, and steam to remove all the fulness. When thoroughly dry, cut the string, remove the wire, and lay the maline circle over the under facing, allowing it to extend out about 1 inch. Pin as at *a*, Fig. 7, lapping it at the back, as at *b*. Stitch it around the edge, as at *c*, and cut away the inner portion of the maline, as at *d*. Then attach the under facing as directed for the top, finishing the outer edge with a cord and slip-stitching the edge of the slashes.

The oval crown is covered plain by drawing all the fulness out on the diagonal points and stitching it around the base. Cut four pointed scallops wide enough to fit the base and extend to the top of the side crown, outline them with a loose-edge cable cord, and apply them to the crown over the diagonal points, as shown in the finished hat on this page.

b

a

Fig. 5

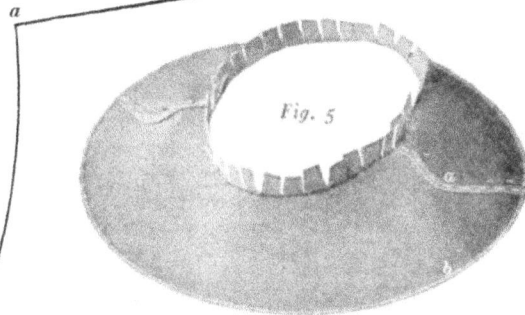

The netine brim after the two sections have been joined and the edge wired.

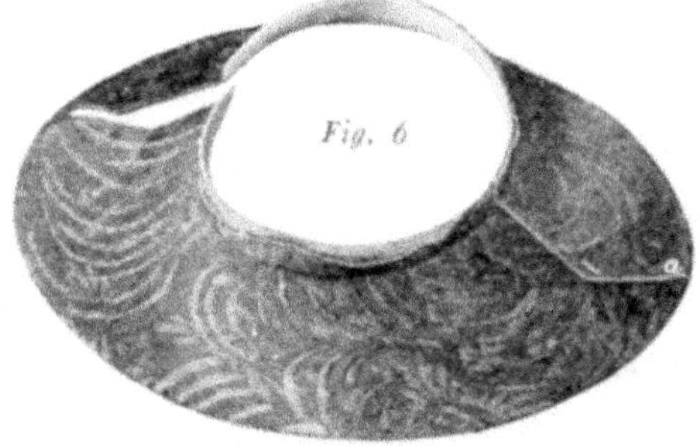

The brim after the brocade has been applied to both sections of the top. Care must be used in making a neat finish where the back section turns over the edge, as at a.

e

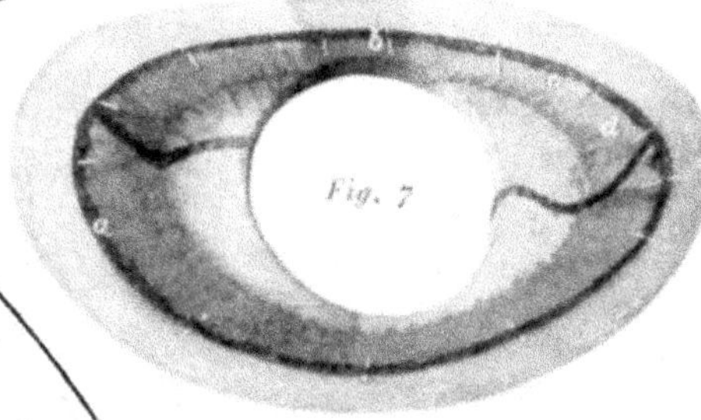

Showing the method of applying the transparent maline flange to the under brim.

When binding the curved edge, cde, of both Figs. 3 and 4, exercise care not to stretch the netine. Much of the success of this model depends on finishing the slashes so that all puckering is avoided.

d

Fig. 2

The outline of one-half the front-brim section. Be sure to place the line ab on the fold of the tissue paper when making the pattern.

A velvet-covered cable cord finishes the base of the crown, and a wreath of metal flowers with ribbon centers extends across the front and through the slashes on the sides, ending on the under brim. The limpness of this brim permits it to be shaped or adjusted to suit the individual style of the wearer. Some desire an easy roll at the left side, while others prefer the brim to droop down on both sides.

c

TRIMMINGS ON FASHION SERVICE MODELS

1.—Shoulder trim used on Model 3D.

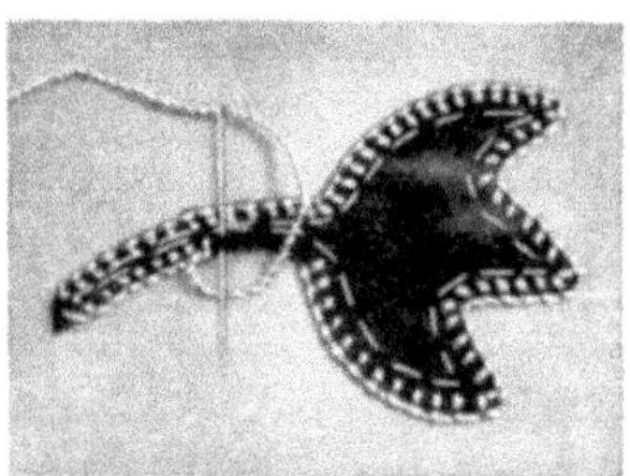

2.—Detail showing velvet appliqué on Model 6B.

3.—Trimming on the front of the center model on Page 39.

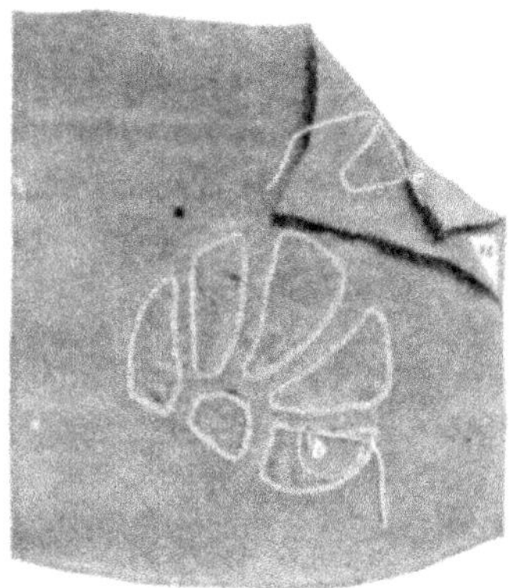

4.—Detail of quilted trimming on Model 6C.

1.—Cut four strips of 1-inch plissé ribbon 4 inches long, round off both ends, gather each strip at the center, apply on top of one another to make the 8-petaled flower, and tack securely. For the tubular leaves and stem, sew together two strips of ½-inch green plissé ribbon and turn right side out.

2.—Cut velvet motifs as shown by means of a paper pattern. Baste these to the dress, and, with heavy embroidery thread, appliqué by means of blanket-stitches about $\frac{1}{16}$ inch deep.

3.—Pale green ribbon run through the material makes the stems, small pieces of yellow ribbon with ends cut diagonally, the flower petals, and yellow and green ribbons, woven in lattice-work effect, the basket of this motif.

4.—Apply a deep fitted facing of self-material to the flounce, leaving the top unattached. Insert one thickness of sheet wadding, 1 inch narrower than the facing, as shown at *a*. Outline the design in chain-stitch, as at *b*, producing a somewhat puffed effect. Slip-stitch the top of the facing to the flounce, as at *c*.

5.—For each petal, use 2 inches of ¾-inch ribbon. Tack the raw ends under and gather one side, as at *a*. Outline a semicircle on the dress with bastings. At one end of this, apply a petal, as at *b*. Lap the next over this, as at *c*, and continue until the outline is complete. Apply another row partly overlapping these, as at *d*. Fill in the entire space.

6.—Face the lower edge of the scalloped skirt with a fitted silk facing, as at *a*. Join two thicknesses of scalloped tulle, sewing the scallops together near the edge, and turn, as at *b*. Place the velvet over the tulle, with scallops even, and catch the straight tulle edge with the slip-stitches that hold the facing, as at *c*.

7.—Picot both edges of a strip of crêpe Elizabeth, ⅜ inch wide, and cut it into 2½-inch lengths for the grapes. Join the ends, gather one edge, and apply each grape to the dress with a French knot at the center. Complete the cluster and make a leaf of a 6-inch strip with outline-stitch for veining. The stems are appliquéd with slip-stitches.

8.—Picot the edge of a strip of material 1 inch wide. Plait it, and stitch along the edge, as at *a*, to hold the plaits. Baste this edge to the edge of the scallops, as at *b*, keeping right sides together. Cut a scalloped facing and place it over the plaited strip so that the plaiting is between it and the dress. Stitch near the edge, as at *c*, turn the scallops right side out, as at *d*, and slip-stitch the facing to the dress, as at *e*.

9.—For each rose, provide a 15-inch length of velvet ribbon 5 inches wide. Join the ends and gather each edge separately. Before drawing them up, cover a millinery wire with silver ribbon, finishing one end with a large knot of ribbon. Draw up the velvet ribbon around the stem so that the knot forms the flower center. Tack the velvet to the silver ribbon, and make loops of the silver ribbon for leaves.

5.—Left—Waist-line trimming of shirred ribbon petals such as is used on Model 3D.

9.—Velvet flower used at waist line of Model 3C.

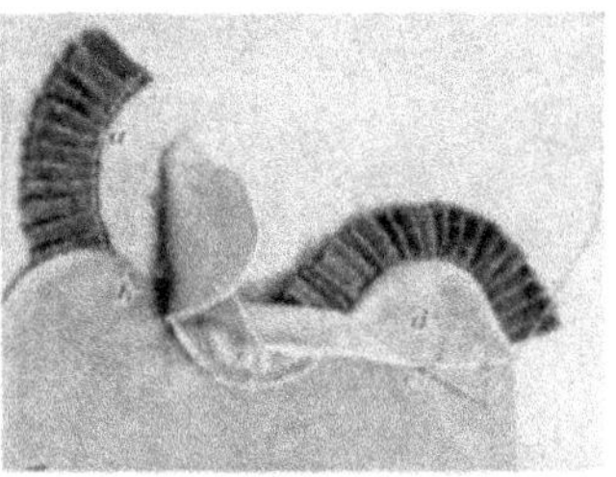

8.—Finishing scallops and applying plaited frills to Model 11C.

7.—The grape motif used as a trimming on Model 11G.

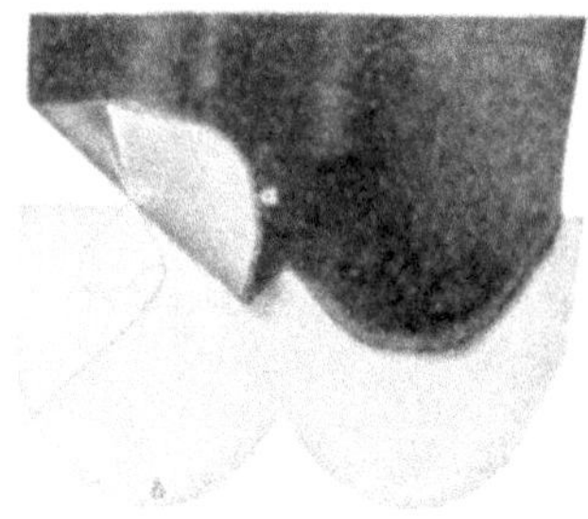

6.—Showing application of tulle scallops to Model 3B.

LINGERIE FEMINIZED BY HAND-WORK

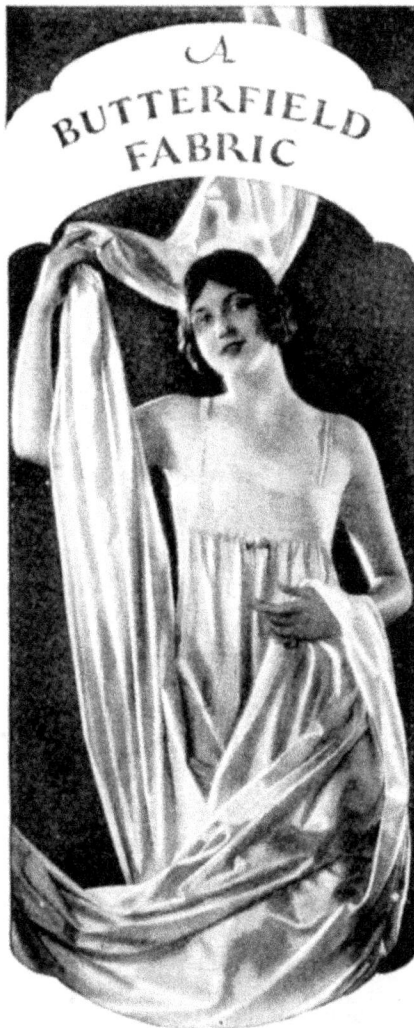

Two-Color Chemise.—Two lengths of fabric so shaped that when seamed together they are an easy fit for the bust at the top and for the hips at the bottom, form the upper section of the chemise shown at the upper left of Page 19. Shape the garment in front in a deep scallop, as shown, using for the lower section the color of the upper portion and a harmonizing shade. Machine-hemstitch these together and to the waist portion, keeping the fulness to the sides.

Finish the top of the chemise with a facing of the contrasting color brought to the right side, binding the bottom with the same color. Sew on the flap and shoulder straps.

Flowered Georgette Chemise.—Two 31-inch lengths of Georgette or voile, a figured over a plain, form the body of the chemise at the upper center. The godets require two 18-inch squares of the fabric, one plain and one figured.

Fold the material through the center lengthwise, selvage edges together, then fold again so the second fold comes a seam's width from the selvage edges. Place the folded material with the selvages toward you, and, from the upper left-hand corner, measure along the cut edges 2½ inches and place a point. From the lower right-hand corner, measure along the selvage edges 14 to 15 inches and place another point. Use these as guides in cutting off a triangular section through the four thicknesses of material. Place the 18-inch squares together, fold on the diagonal, and cut on this line.

Join the two thicknesses of material in a single under-arm seam, and insert the godets with machine-hemstitching after rounding off the points. These come to within 2½ inches of the bottom of the garment, the amount below forming the flap. Finish the edges of the flap with machine-hemstitching and sew the two free edges together with a French seam. Finish the top of the chemise with a 2-inch hemstitched hem, picot or bind the lower edges of the godets, and apply ribbon or self-fabric shoulder straps.

Chemise With Net Trimming.—Two straight lengths of material, one a full width, the other a half or third, depending on one's size, are needed for the chemise shown at the upper right. Shape the full width, trimming from it a section 14 inches long and wide enough to make its upper edge correspond to the bust measure plus 2 to 3 inches, the extra amount to be taken up in pin tucks.

For a dart, slash from the bottom of this cut-out section toward the center front about 5 inches, gathering the lower edge of the dart and attaching it to the upper edge in a French seam. Join the under-arm seams, leaving them open for 12 to 14 inches from the bottom.

Finish the top of the chemise with a double thickness of scalloped net and the lower edge with footing. Place vertical tucks 4 inches long and ⅛ inch deep to emphasize the waist line.

Nightgown With Flower Motif.—To make the nightgown at the lower left, provide one and one-half widths of material in the proper length and sew together.

Fold so that the seams come together, considering the center of the wide section as the center front and that of the narrow as the center back. Place your cutting guide, which should be a foundation waist pattern, in the usual way, having the armholes exactly opposite each other. Cut the outline of the neck, back and front, as well as the armholes. Do not cut the under-arm line but cut straight across from the top of one under arm to the other, leaving the excess material to be arranged in a box plait.

Join the shoulders with French seams and finish the neck and lower edge of the gown with bias binding. Arrange the inverted box plaits at the under arms, catching the edges only at the under-arm seam. Before hand-stitching the armhole binding, turn under the top edges of both plaits and whip together.

The appliqué consists merely of circles and shaped pieces, applied with outline-stitches taken on the edges and continued to provide the decorative lines shown.

Costume Slip.—But 2 yards of 40-inch silk are required for the slip at the lower center. Cut off ½ yard, and use the remainder for the slip proper, cutting it on the cross of the fabric and arranging the fulness below the dart line in tucks on the wrong side.

Turn a 2-inch hem at the top and finish the bottom with a 12-inch facing by cutting the extra ½ yard of fabric into strips of this width and joining them. Make the appliqué of dull and lustrous silks in varying tones of one color.

Applique-Trimmed Nightgown.—For the nightgown at the lower left, supply a width and a half of material, following the directions for cutting and sewing the nightgown at the lower right. Apply the appliqué, a motif over each shoulder and over each plait at a low waist line. Attach the unturned edges with fine blanket-stitches, and if necessary to keep the motif smooth, use blanket-stitches through the center, following the line of the design. Leave a small space through which to run the ribbon belt. A gown of this type would be lovely of lingette with appliqué of voile flowers.

The 3 Points of Perfection

You find them all combined only *in*

PICTORIAL REVIEW PRINTED PATTERNS

1 *Printed* - Easy-to-follow instructions printed on the clear, clean tissue paper.

2 *Perforated* - Accurate perforations show where to mark *through* pattern. This simplifies putting the garment together.

3 *Cut Out* - Every pattern piece is cut out and ready to use. No margins to trim away or mislead you. The material is always in sight as you cut along the scientifically accurate edge.

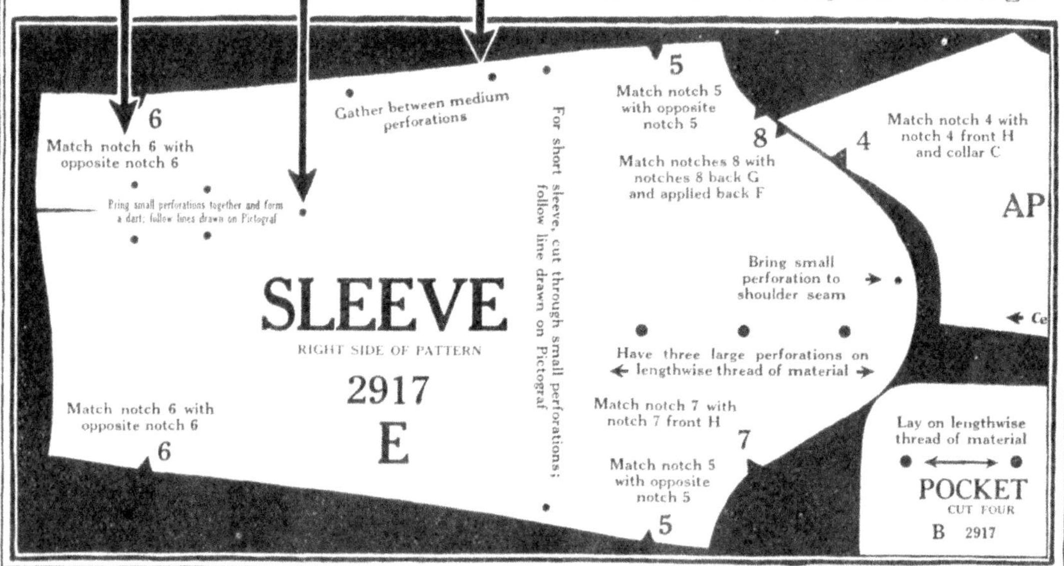

Sold by Leading Dealers Everywhere

THE PICTORIAL REVIEW COMPANY

Seventh Avenue and 39th Street

NEW YORK CITY

VOLUME 1
225 Pages
74 Illustrations
VOLUME 2
211 Pages
72 Illustrations
VOLUME 3
243 Pages
156 Illustrations
VOLUME 4
245 Pages
127 Illustrations
VOLUME 5
303 Pages
97 Illustrations

"We have gone with particular care through the five-volume Woman's Institute Library of Cookery. I know of no other one source equal to it to which a woman could go for every kind of information she could conceivably need on the subject of cookery."
ELIZABETH MCDONALD, *Modern Priscilla.*

Salient Facts About the Library of Cookery

—1,227 Pages, 526 Illustrations.
—Embodies, in book form, a complete comprehensive Course in Foods and Cookery.
—Every recipe thoroughly tested and tried out in our own model kitchen.
—Endorsed by editors, school authorities, and others competent to judge as exceptionally authoritative work.
—More than 75,000 volumes distributed.

Your Christmas Gift Problem Solved

One Set for Yourself---One for Your Friend

HERE is a happy solution to the gift problem—five wonderful volumes filled with health and happiness. Think of the pleasure you will bring your friends with these lovely volumes—perhaps a set complete to some dearly loved one, or perhaps a volume each to five friends to whom these gifts would mean so much (yes, you can break up the set; each volume is complete in itself and would therefore make an exceptionally acceptable gift).

The Famous Woman's Institute LIBRARY OF COOKERY

Here is the complete Woman's Institute Course in Foods and Cookery (without correspondence instruction), now published for your convenience in five handsome volumes, beautifully bound in long-wearing, delft blue cloth, stamped in gold, 1,227 pages, 526 illustrations.

Do not think of these books as cook books. They contain, it is true, more than 1,000 tried, tested, proved recipes, but unlike any cook book you ever saw, they give you graphic step-by-step directions for making everything. Not alone *how* but WHY you do it. So, as you learn to prepare each article of food for the table, you learn also its food value, its composition, its place in the diet.

SEND NO MONEY---Examine for 5 Days Free!

Best of all, you need send no money. Simply fill in and mark (or copy the wording of) the coupon below. The complete Library of five volumes will be sent to you at once. When you receive the books, examine them at your leisure, keep them for five full days, then if you are satisfied they are exactly as represented and that you want their help in your kitchen, send only $3 as your first payment and $3 each month for four more months until $15 has been paid. Or, if you wish, you may deduct 10%, sending only $13.50 in full payment.

On the other hand, if for any reason you are not completely satisfied that the books are worth far more than this small cost, return them and you will not be under the slightest further obligation.

— — — — — — TEAR OUT HERE — — — — — —

Book Department 999, Woman's Institute, Scranton, Pa.

Yes, indeed, I would like to have you send the wonderful five-volume Library of Cookery to me for five days' free examination. It is understood that if I am not completely satisfied I may return the books without obligation of any sort. If I am completely satisfied the books are what you say—and even more—I will keep them, and send $3.00 within five days as an initial payment, and $3.00 per month for four months. (Or, if paid at once, $13.50—a further discount of 10 per cent.)

*Name*______________________________

Street Address ______________________________

*City*____________________*State*____________

*Class Letter and No.*__________________________

Magic Pattern: Flat-wash Nightie

This is an original Magic Pattern, a project you cut out using diagrams instead of pattern pieces. These were first created by Mary Brooks Picken for the Woman's Institute's student magazines, Inspiration and Fashion Service. My book **Vintage Notions: An Inspirational Guide to Needlework, Cooking, Sewing, Fashion & Fun** *featured 12 original Magic Patterns. Recently I have created modern patterns that were inspired by these vintage gems featured in the book* **The Magic Pattern Book**, *which I licensed with Workman Publishing. We have chosen to keep the authenticity of this original pattern intact and therefore have not changed instructions based on modern fabrics and techniques. Note at the end of this pattern you will find helpful tips for drafting pattern pieces.*

▶▶▶A JOY TO IRON, this nightie. Just run it flat through the ironer, or send it to wet-wash laundry. No fussing with ruffles or gathers—lace trim lies flat. It is comfortable to sleep in, too. Make it of cotton plissé crepe, of batiste, or of any soft, lightweight cotton, or, for winter, of cotton flannel. Buy two lengths, shoulder to floor, plus 1 in. for hem, and 2¼ yds. of Irish-type crochet lace.

Straighten ends of fabric. For ties, tear a 2-in. strip from one selvage. Clip or tear off other selvage. Fold material in half lengthwise. Pin edges together. Mark center with pin on fold (*A* in diagram) and on raw edges (*B*). Measure in from *A* one-third of the neck measurement, then on fold 2 in. to left of *A* and 6 in. to right. Mark curves and cut back and front neckline.

Measure 10 in. from *B* for *C*. Directly across on fold mark *D*. Measure from *D* one-fourth bust measurement plus 4 in. (*E*).

Measure 20 in. to left of corner *F* for G. Connect *C*, *E*, and *G*, making curved underarm, as shown. Cut on this line for front. Fold over on back along shoulder line (*A*), and cut back underarm to correspond to front.

On sleeve and neck edge turn a narrow hem, stitch to wrong side, baste lace in place under hem, and stitch. Begin at underarm seam for sleeves and on one shoulder for neck. Shape lace around curve, join in narrow seam, then overcast ends to prevent fraying.

To make center-stitched ties, turn in on both ends. Fold raw edge over a scant one-third of the width of the strip, and fold selvage over a scant one-third. Stitch through center for full length of strip. Cut tie strip in half.

Mark waistline with pin. Four in. each side of center-front make a ½-in. tuck 1½ in. long. Stitch tie ends on, as at *H*. Fold tuck toward side seam; stitch again, as at *I*.

Beginning at bottom of sleeves, French-seam underarms and sides, finishing about 12 in. above hem. Make narrow hems on these open edges. Stitch these across seam at end to prevent tearing. Turn and stitch 1-in. hem along bottom edges.

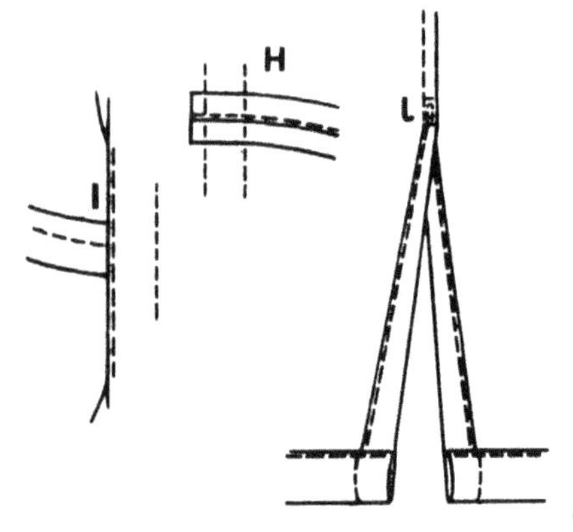

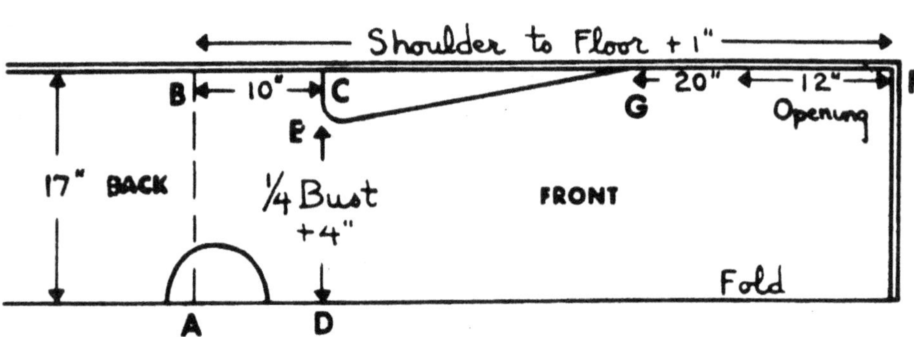

Tailored Smartness in Frocks of GILBRAE
FALL and winter fashions, youthful, colorful, and so frequently of tailored smartness, can be charmingly expressed in frocks of GILBRAE. For this lovely cotton fabric is of such firm and even texture that it tailors as neatly and stitches as perfectly as a piece of fine wool.
Made of yarn dyed cotton, woven slowly and with infinite care, GILBRAE comes from the loom a soft and dainty fabric that invites the needle. And since its tempting variety of distinctive patterns are absolutely fast color, it can be laundered as easily as a linen handkerchief.
Best of all, GILBRAE is surprisingly inexpensive. So from the time you choose the material at the counter, through the making, the wearing, and repeated tubbings, a dress of GILBRAE is a source of enduring satisfaction.
Amory, Browne & Co.
Box 1206, BOSTON, MASS.
Indian Head Cloth
Buster Brown Hosiery
Nashua Part Wool Blankets
Conestogo Woven Tickings
Kalburnie Ginghams
Parkhill Ginghams
GILBRAE fine COTTONS

Vintage advertisment from Fashion Services Winter 1925-1926

THE ART OF GIVING

By CLARICE CARPENTER
Department of Dressmaking

CHRISTMAS giving is something more than a lovely custom. It is an art—a fine art which you have mastered when your gifts are individual and thoughtful and fitted to the needs of those to whom they are given. The gifts shown here serve to illustrate the point.

Out of the sympathetic understanding of a little girl's longing for beauty in that most precious of places, her *own* room, grew the plan for the simple unbleached muslin bedspread and curtains at the upper left. Bands of checked gingham, $1\frac{1}{2}$ inches wide, in her favorite color are applied. The edges are finished with rickrack of the same color.

A bride who loves pretty things but does not have "a knack with the needle" was delighted with the two aprons of unbleached muslin. Very simple embroidery stitches trim the one at the left. The one at the right is decorated with cotton-crêpe flowers in blue, yellow, and gold whipped down with sewing thread.

Three lengths of coral pink and a half yard of sea-blue crêpe de Chine will make a gown and a slip for the "very best friend." Each has a half width inserted in the back.

A college girl would appreciate either the tan duvetyn scarf trimmed with ribbon in shades of brown and tan for sports wear, or the orchid chiffon one with trimming loops of violet ribbon for wear with the dance frocks.

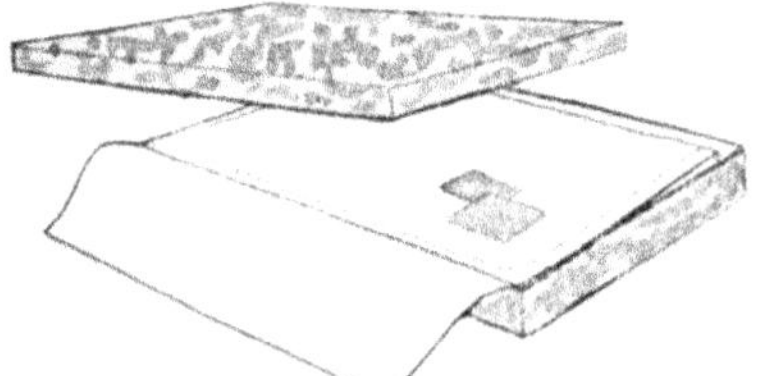

AT the upper right is a pair of dainty curtains for the bathroom window of a friend who has a brand new house. They are made of striped dimity, edged with narrow lace, and embroidered in a very simple design.

Soft warm blankets with ribbon-bound ends are an ideal gift for an invalid friend. The perky bow will surely cause enforced rest periods to seem less distasteful.

Any housekeeper will welcome a half dozen dish towels, and will take great pride in the air of distinction they give her kitchen when one corner of each is decorated with two 2-inch squares of gingham in contrasting colors. Those at the right are made from flour sacks.

A comfort-top protector of white lawn decorated with French knots is a thoughtful gift and inexpensive.

TWO pieces of linen joined on three edges with crocheting form a pocket for the piece of heavy cardboard that transforms them into a hot-dish mat. The open end is held in place with snaps. Three or four make a set.

A bit of material and an hour's time will make a One Hour dress that means Merry Christmas to some otherwise giftless little girl.

Scraps of silk crêpe from summer dresses make lovely gay ties for the schoolgirl's tailored frock with an accompanying linen collar.

A card-table cover that stays on is made of black sateen and has ribbon bands through which weighted tape is run.

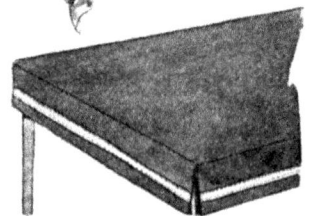

Freshening Your *Winter* Frocks

By ALICE SEIPP
Art Department

At the turn of the year, when a winter wardrobe loses its freshness and spring is still around the corner, one welcomes the trifles that work such subtle changes in frocks. It takes only a tiny neck finish sometimes, such as are shown on this page, a simple sleeve trim, or a unique belt arrangement to change the character of a dress entirely and to bring it definitely up to date.

Left—The round neck line and the surplice closing, shown here, have been treated attractively. To the former has been applied a deep collar of fine batiste or Georgette edged with cream duchesse lace and trimmed with tiny pearl buttons. A fold of tan grosgrain silk outlines the latter and buttons with three self-covered buttons.

Right—The Dutch collar and gauntlet cuffs of cream net with Val and filet lace add a charming note to a plain frock. The V neck line of a jersey dress might be finished with a stitched yoke of matching crêpe de Chine and a made flower.

Above—A V neck line may be finished with a bit of novelty ribbon fagoted on, several strips of the ribbon being tied at the joining.

On a crêpe dress, a matching satin may be used, the ends of the knotted tie finished with embroidery of self-color and metal thread, and a shaped section inserted in the blouse.

Right Above—The small collar-and-cuff set are of plaid taffeta and brown satin with tiny gold buttons as trim.

The batiste vestee, tucked and trimmed with lace, makes a pleasing finish for a dress with a low neck line.

Center—A dainty batiste collar and plaited jabot are trimmed with Val lace and edged with bias binding in a contrasting color. Tiny colored novelty buttons finish the front.

Above—An old-fashioned sleeve may be made modish with lace and velvet or satin, as shown in the two finishes to the left.

The three-tiered sleeve finish is made of two folds of dark silk and one of white satin or piqué.

For a dress of crêpe Elizabeth, the waist-line and cuff finish of velvet at the right, with its bow ties of the crêpe Elizabeth, offers a unique trimming for an otherwise simple dress.

Above—A high collar of crêpe de Chine uses écru Georgette for its small turn-over collar and jabot, the edge of the latter being scalloped and finished with a binding of the crêpe de Chine, which matches the dress.

An organdie vestee, with ruffles of self-material, makes a smart accessory for a bolero.

Left Above—The draped bertha of Georgette is edged on each side with a contrasting ribbon and uses filigree buttons as a trim.

A collar and vestee made of two shades of reseda crêpe de Chine and buckle-trimmed may be inserted in a sports dress or blouse of jersey or crepella.

Left—To bring an old short-sleeved dress up to date, a deep cape-like sleeve of contrasting material may be added, sewed together from elbow to wrist.

A Magic Cover-All Apron

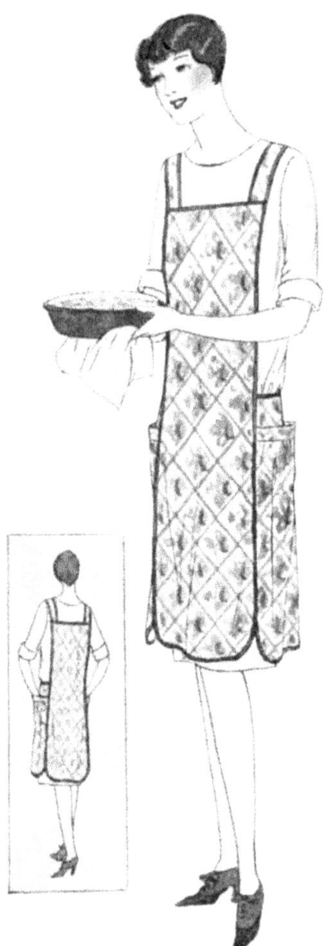

A FEW straight pieces of fabric, a few yards of bias tape, an hour or so of time, and presto! a cover-all apron that will make housekeeping a joy! It's attractive, practical, and economical of material—1¾ yards of fabric and 8 to 9 yards of bias tape being all that's needed. A print in cretonne design, with trimming matching the dominant color is smart; but, if desired, a combination of plain and figured fabrics may be used, the front panels of the plain material and the sides of the print, an excellent plan when making use of two short lengths of material.

FOR the average figure, 32-inch material is satisfactory; but when the figure is stout, it is well to supply a 36-inch width. For the slender figure, when 36-inch material is used, trim away a 4-inch strip throughout its full length.

The accompanying diagram makes cutting easy. Straighten the ends of material if they are not already straight. Then fold through the center lengthwise and place on the table with the fold next you. To get the front and back sections, measure from the lower right corner to the left a distance equal to the length you wish the apron to be, for the average figure 36 inches. Trim off this section on a straight line. Then trim off triangular sections, as shown, cutting on each side from a point 2 inches from the edge to a point 18 inches from the end along both the fold and the selvage. This narrows the pieces at the top. Cut along the fold to separate the sections.

From the large section remaining, trim off a portion measuring 22 inches in length for the side panels, also cutting along the fold to make two panels of equal size. Along the selvage, cut off two shoulder straps, each 2 inches wide.

Cut the pocket foundations from the section remaining, making them 11 inches wide and as deep as the material will allow, which should be about 8 inches. The remaining strip will permit of cutting the two pocket bands, which should each be 2½ inches wide, their length to be determined later when you have decided on the finished width of the side panels.

PIN the shoulder straps in place and slip the apron on with front and back in proper position. Then pin the foundation pockets in place, arranging them so that the apron fits easily around the hips and their upper edges come at about the normal waist line. This will usually mean that the pocket sections will be wider at the bottom than at the top. Remove the apron and pin the side panels in place to obtain their correct length, starting at the bottom. If they seem long, trim them off at the top the necessary amount. Gather to a size that measures 2 inches greater than the width of the pocket foundation and bind with the straight strips provided for this purpose. Shape the lower edges of these as well as the front and back sections, as shown.

Bind the lower edges of both side panels and the upper edges of the pocket foundations. Then gather the side panels to fit the lower edges of these foundations, baste in place, and stitch, thus forming pockets.

Bind the front and back pieces and the shoulder straps. Then baste the finished side sections in place and stitch just beyond the binding. With the apron on, pin the shoulder straps in place, and then attach them securely.

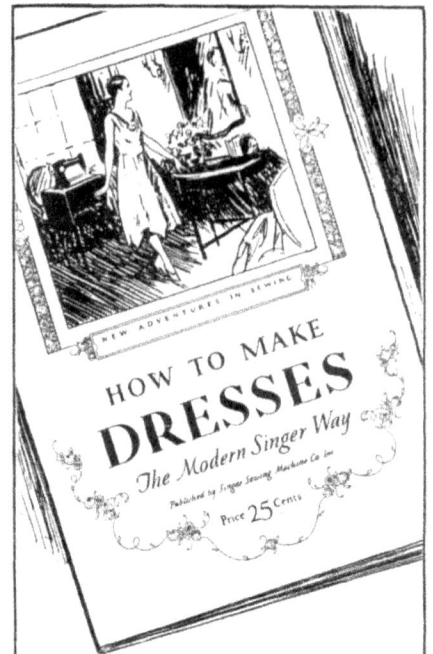

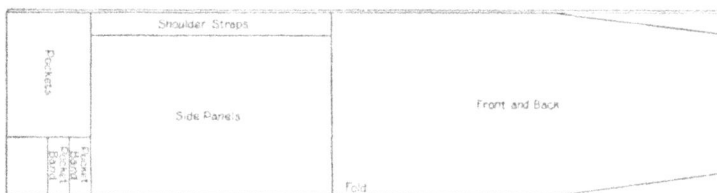

From Fashion Services Winter, 1928

Vintage Notions Monthly continues to share the work of Mary Brooks Picken and the Woman's Institute which inspired my book *Vintage Notions*. Although the Institute was founded 100 years ago, the treasure trove of lessons and stories are still relevant today and offer a blueprint for living a contented life.

If you enjoyed this issue of *Vintage Notions Monthly*, visit AmyBarickman.com for more of my curated collection of vintage content including patterns and books for needle and thread, inspiring fabric and textiles & free vintage art every Friday. Be sure to tune in to *Vintage Notions* episodes for a guided tour through my collection of sewing and fashion history, as well as modern projects inspired by my extensive library.

www.amybarickman.com

Find free images, inspiration and books for the sewing and needle arts!

www.indygojunction.com

Featuring digital & print patterns, books, tutorials, giveaways, project ideas, & more!

Subscribe to each of our eNewsletters to learn about new products, receive special offers, discounts, videos, and get a FREE eBook!

Vintage Notions Monthly, Issue 24 (VN0212)

For wholesale ordering information contact Amy Barickman, LLC at 913.341.5559
or amyb@amybarickman.com, P.O. Box 30238, Kansas City, MO 64112

www.ingramcontent.com/pod-product-compliance
Lightning Source LLC
LaVergne TN
LVHW061331060426
835513LV00015B/1359
* 9 7 8 1 9 4 6 0 9 8 1 3 9 *

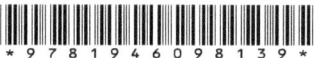